SPIRIT OF AMERICANA
Life Lived in the American Spirit

James Carl Anderson, author
Polly Purnell, co-author/editor

authorHOUSE®

AuthorHouse™
1663 Liberty Drive
Bloomington, IN 47403
www.authorhouse.com
Phone: 1-800-839-8640

First published by AuthorHouse 7/12/2011

ISBN: 978-1-4567-5381-8 (sc)
ISBN: 978-1-4567-5403-7 (hc)
ISBN: 978-1-4567-5380-1 (e)

Library of Congress Control Number: 2011908038

Printed in the United States of America

FOREWORD

Spirit of Americana presents a sometimes humorous, sometimes serious, scenario of rural communities, especially "The Ridge" in middle Tennessee. This book explains how such a setting can promote freedom and democracy, especially in America, and possibly in other countries as well.

Spectators were entertained watching a tug of war between "Old Jack," a big mule, and a new 1935 Ford coupe. Many of the same people were saddened a few months later when the contest sponsor and his mother died the same day of pneumonia, an epidemic rampaging through The Ridge. Twin coffins were hauled to a hillside graveyard on a flat bed log truck.

How did this widow and her seven little children survive the great depression of the 1930's?

Since making moonshine whiskey was illegal in the 1930's, how did federal, state and county law enforcement officers cut down a huge still on Moonshine Island without making a single arrest?

Furthermore, how did one of the nation's most wanted criminals serve as a deputy sheriff in the same community in later years?

Spirit of Americana provides some logical answers to these puzzling questions.

Necessity being the mother of invention explains how a resident of this poverty stricken ridge harnessed his waterfall to generate electricity for his home using automobile and bicycle parts. The Tennessee Valley Authority (TVA) and the Rural Electrical Association (REA) followed this same method a few years later bringing electricity from huge dams and generators to many houses on The Ridge and elsewhere.

The Ridge did not lack military heroes during two World Wars, as well as wars in Korea, Vietnam, Kuwait, Iraq, and Afghanistan. Some came home alive. Some did not. Freedom was not cheap. The Ridge residents believed in America maintaining its freedom.

Some of the poorest elementary schools in Tennessee and possibly in the U.S. were located on The Ridge during the great depression of the 1930's and early 1940's evidenced by the school not passing inspection because of its outhouse (toilet) causing students not to be eligible for high school. One young man protested and graduated four years later as the outstanding student among the 350 students of the school.

Colonel George Patton (later General George C. Patton) led his Army into Middle Tennessee during World War II to train for war against, perhaps, the best German Army ever. Some of the poorest youngsters on The Ridge served as spies for Patton's soldiers from a tree house using a crude communications system and being rewarded with camping supplies as well as chocolate candy and "K" rations.

"Spirit of Americana" describes a church group debate that took place the same year as "Brown vs. School Board of Topeka." The decisions of the U.S. Supreme Court and the college debate judges were the same. Today's residents of The Ridge will recognize this church as one that met under two pine trees until a brick building was completed.

The "Fourth and One" chapter describes how one of Tennessee's best football teams wore white jerseys, played with a white football, featured a large marching band, and lost to a young inexperienced team that had no band! The little team did have a bunch of "Scots" from The Ridge.

This book includes an original country song that has made grown men cry and children dance at the same time. A soloist has tested the song at family reunions, family groups, assisted living facilities, and retirement homes.

The "Spirit of Americana" was, indeed, tested when a teacher from Boston, Massachusetts, conversed with a grist mill operator on The Ridge. He asked the teacher a "Spirit-related" question. She gave him an "Americana-motivated" answer. This book, and only this book, reveals the personal circumstances involved in that conversation. The miller learned a lesson and the teacher learned to respect the down-to-earth intelligence of a grist mill operator who was also a blacksmith.

ABOUT THE AUTHOR

James Carl Anderson showed a great deal of interest in the fine arts while in high school. For example, he was a member of the high school choir, President of his senior class, President of the Beta Club, and played a lead role in a Beta Club play. He also helped the Carter Family (Mother May Belle, sister, Sarah, and daughters, June and Anita) perform a concert at Jackson County Central High School in his senior year.

While attending Tennessee Tech (1950-1954), Anderson was the student librarian of the college athletic library. He helped edit the "Tennessee Teach Homespun" magazine and sold ads to finance the project. Anderson improved his speaking and writing ability while debating some very important issues. His speeches, while in a dress Rural Officer Training Corps (ROTC) uniform, helped Tennessee Tech reach and surpass its stated goal.

Perhaps Anderson's most useful writing was accomplished when he served as Exhibits Manager for Oak Ridge Associated Universities in Oak Ridge, Tennessee. He played a key role in writing "This Atomic World." In addition, he presented the 45-minute high school assembly program, based on the script, more than 1000 times across the United States of America.

He spent four summers at the University of Colorado in Boulder, Colorado, while employed at Oak Ridge, and wrote a professional report, "A Study of Evaluating the Effectiveness of High School Assemblies." A summary of that report was published in "Student Activities Magazine" in 1963.

As an employee of Combustion Engineering, Inc., in Windsor, Connecticut, Anderson helped world-renowned scientists write and prepare videotapes of two training programs, "Introduction to Nuclear

Power" and "Introduction to Environmental Protection" (40 hrs. and 20 hrs. respectively). The sales department training program helped the company reach $2,000,000,000 in sales of nuclear steam supply systems and clean-up systems for coal-burning electrical power plants.

Perhaps his greatest impact on society during a 50-year career in the military, industrial, and educational fields was when he served as Supervisor of Adult Education for Jackson County, Tennessee. He also doubled as the Assistant Football Coach for twelve years.

During those 20 years, Anderson wrote approximately 100 feature articles for the Jackson County Sentinel that described the Friday night games of the local high school football team.

Anderson also prepared more than 1000 lesson plans related to English, mathematics, social studies, history, creative writing, and science. His professional report on adult education helped him earn an Ed.S Degree at Tennessee Tech.

"Spirit of Americana," gave the author a chance to recall some of the most fascinating, funny, fulfilling, educational, and, yes, sad experiences of a lifetime. The author said, "Some of those events of the 1930's are clearer in my mind now than some experiences of 2010." However, these book-worthy events were never printed until he sat down to write "Spirit of Americana."

JAMES CARL ANDERSON

James Carl Anderson in Spring of 1954 stands proudly beside his 1930 Ford Model –A Roadster at Tennessee Tech University just after winning the Ohio Valley Conference Championship in the high jump contest and setting a new conference record. The roadster led the school parade with 10 student passengers.

While attending Tennessee Tech, he worked during summers at Chrysler Corporation and General Motors in Detroit, Michigan, and United Engineers, Inc., in Marine City, Michigan, to pay for his Roadster and college expenses.

ABOUT THE CO-AUTHOR
AND EDITOR

Polly Betty (Anderson) Purnell is the youngest daughter of Robert (Bob) Benjamin Anderson and Rose Lee (Pharris) Anderson. Polly was born three months after the death of Polly Birdwell Anderson, Robert's mother. Bob's mother's death was caused by the epidemic that ravaged the community which also caused the death of her son, Bedford Anderson. Robert Anderson decided to give this child his mother's name in honor of one who was so dearly loved and greatly missed.

Polly always enjoyed public speaking and acting. As early as third grade she attempted to write plays and would "show off" by reading aloud to the class because she was the fastest reader. One day she read so fast she skipped a word and was embarrassed to be seated while someone else was given the honor of reading aloud. She was promoted from first grade to third grade with 5 other children in the small country school she attended. This caused her to always be the youngest in her classes, but did not suppress her scholastic abilities.

Polly graduated from Oak Ridge High School, a member of the National Honor Society, where she participated in plays at the school. She went on to graduate from Business College in Knoxville, Tennessee, the only child in her family to be educated past high school.

Her employment included the Department of Energy's (DOE) predecessor in Oak Ridge, Tennessee, in administrative positions. Later as a DOE subcontractor employee, she held positions of editorial significance and assisted in the maintenance and publication of DOE contract appendices. Polly greatly enjoyed participation in Toastmasters during these years at DOE, honing her public speaking and writing skills, while forming friendships lasting to this day.

Polly traveled to various distant locations with her husband, William (Bill) Purnell, while he pursued his military career. They parented five children, who blessed them with nine grandchildren, and five great-grandchildren.

Being a co-author and editor to "Spirit of Americana" has been a labor of love inspired by the words of the song, "TWIN COFFINS." Polly first wrote a chapter about the circumstances surrounding that song and that chapter prompted James Carl Anderson to encourage her to write a book with his assistance. Little did they realize that the story would unfold to be a microcosm of American living that so many people experienced during the 1930s and following years. James Carl's life was the story of so many families living and working during those years. This one man's life story was lived in the "Spirit of Americana."

POLLY PURNELL, CO-AUTHOR AND EDITOR

Polly Betty (Anderson) Purnell is the youngest daughter of Robert (Bob) Benjamin Anderson and Rose Lee (Pharris) Anderson. Polly was born three months after the death of Polly Birdwell Anderson, Robert's mother. "Ma" Anderson's death was caused by the pneumonia and influenza epidemic that ravaged the community. Robert Anderson gave his youngest child his mother's name in honor of one who was so dearly loved and greatly missed.

ACKNOWLEDGEMENTS

The authors are indebted to James Carl's parents, James Bedford Anderson and Lola (Loftis) Anderson, as well as Polly Purnell's parents, Robert Benjamin Anderson and Rose Lee (Pharris) Anderson, for the principles of honesty, integrity, hard work, and charity toward others taught and demonstrated to their children. The authors are appreciative of their siblings' lives enacting these highly regarded character qualities. The lives described in this book were repeated across America during the years the principle characters lived and these qualities were admired, expected of others, and respected by all.

We wish to thank Mike Anderson of Bellrica, Massachusetts, for helping to write the chapter, "My Family Visited The Ridge."

We are grateful to Nell Cowan of Gainesboro, Tennessee, for assistance with word processing, editing, and gathering materials for the original manuscript.

Our thanks are extended to Jewel Lee (Anderson) Whitaker and Nathaniel Chambers, husband of Polly's sister, Reba, for their thoughtful contributions of events in the young lives of Robert Benjamin Anderson's children.

We wholeheartedly appreciate the able assistance provided by Lisa Kincaid in preparing photographs for publication.

Chris Roberts and his studio staff in Cookeville, Tennessee, are to be highly commended for providing guitar lessons, content editing of songs, and encouragement related to "Spirit of Americana."

Last, but not least, the former teachers and students of Jackson County Central High School and historic elementary schools, McCoinsville, Dudney's Hill, Center Grove, New Salem, Antioch and Flynn's Lick shall long be remembered for their educational, economic, leadership, and spiritual contributions made to their communities, Tennessee, and America. What happened on The Ridge demonstrated "Rags to Riches" at its very best. The rural school system played a very positive role.

We, the authors of "Spirit of Americana," offer our sincere thanks to everyone who helped create the story told in this little book.

CONTENTS

CONTENTS

TWIN COFFINS

They sat side by side on the grass under the box elder tree in the front yard of the house, made of planed poplar planks; the outside covered by grey cloth and the inside lined with a white covering lovingly sewn and placed there by a dear cousin. The house was embraced by a porch on three sides built by James Carl's daddy for his bride of just 20 years before his death took him from her. These embracing porches were wide enough for the family to sit on and talk to passing neighbors, run around with cousins, and keep an eye on the crops in the fields nearby. The sun was shining on that spring day; the trees were beginning to green out; and flowers were blooming by the road side. It was a time of forsythia, daffodils, and red bud trees. In a nearby orchard fruit trees grew in abundance.

They sat there under the tree side by side, newly nailed together, holding the bodies of these two loved ones no one could believe were truly gone. James Carl had felt grass on his bare feet in the back yard just the day before, watching while planks were laid on sawhorses and nailed together. One was for his daddy whose arms could embrace like the porch of his home. This house would now shelter his mother and her seven children without his daddy's laughter flowing through the rooms. His daddy, in whose home relatives were invited to visit or maybe stay overnight, was placed in one of those twin coffins in the front yard of his home. The other one was for his father's mother, James Carl's grandmother. In James Carl's four-year old mind, he could not realize the lonely days that were to come and what the absence of his daddy would mean to him and his mother. Headstones were also homemade in those days, made from purchased sand. If these are found today, they have usually crumbled or chipped.

Every member of the family had this terrible illness except for James

Carl and two of his older sisters. His mother was near death herself. While the funeral was held on the front lawn, she could barely raise herself from her bed to watch out the window; her strawberry blonde hair falling around her grieving eyes, not strong enough to go out to the yard or to the cemetery.

Ma Polly, James Carl's grandmother, lay side by side with her son, both so recently taken by this plague that caused breathing to be impossibly hard and then cease altogether. Ma Polly, as James Carl called her, always had sweet, good-tasting gingerbread with a cold glass of milk to give to grandchildren to enjoy.

THOMAS AND POLLY ANDERSON
GRANDPARENTS OF
JAMES CARL ANDERSON AND POLLY PURNELL

After the service in the front yard, those twin coffins were placed in the back of a family friend's new orange truck and taken to the cemetery to be placed in freshly dug graves. James Carl and two of his sisters rode in a car behind, in shock and disbelief, the floorboard hot under their feet.

His grandmother died one afternoon at two o'clock and his daddy died that night at two in the morning of this double pneumonia plague that had spread through the community like wildfire. His daddy had, a few weeks before, helped another family carry out three of their own to be placed in coffins, having suffered the same fate. Even the special treatment of drinking sulfur water provided by their trustworthy doctor, given a few days prior to his death, did not stop this rampant epidemic from ravaging this home with the loss of the husband and father.

James Carl's father had, a few months before falling ill, faced off a threat to the family's property. A neighbor made a wagon and sled road across his father's corn/hay field. His dad and his older brothers were building a fence on the surveyed line. The neighbor became furious, got his gun, his wife screamed at him, and he did not shoot. A few months later, when James Carl's father was dying with pneumonia, the neighbor came to his bedside and apologized.

In those days coffins were made at home from lumber of surrounding timber, sometimes cherry or poplar, sometimes pine. Neighbors came to help build them and place them to hold the bodies. Neighbors helped dig the graves and the family filled the holes back up covering the coffins.

LUMBER FOR THE TWIN COFFINS WAS STORED IN THE LOFT OF THIS LATE 19TH CENTURY BARN

This old barn was built by Tom Anderson and his sons
in the late 19th century and still stands today. It stored
lumber for coffins, corn and hay for mules and cows,
a hillside plow for farming, and some blacksmith tools.
One side of the barn had rooms (stalls) for animals.

Before the loved ones were placed in the prepared coffins, it was the custom to have them "laid out" and family and neighbors sat with them for a time. James Carl's father had a rented house before he built the main house. The main house was used for the viewings of loved ones. Viewings for children, for young men, for parents and grandparents were held there. The rented house had burned and he built the main house that still stands today as well as a smokehouse. Some say it is just wild animals or the wind that makes the sad, mourning sounds of lonesomeness that are sometimes heard around the main house.

After the cemetery ceremony, all who attended were invited to come back to the house and eat food prepared and provided. The conversation was of memories of those loved ones just departed, sometimes a good memory with a laugh, sometimes a good memory of kind and decent actions taken, sometimes a sad memory of the suffering they had gone through and suffering yet to come because they were gone.

James Carl would always remember his dad was one who helped so many others in that community, whatever the needs might be. He helped with planting, harvesting, building, and all those actions needed to maintain life and family in his day. One time when he was digging post holes, he held James Carl by his ankles and lowered him down into the hole to rake out the rocks and debris. He was quick to take James Carl with him to the store for candy and soda pop.

James Carl remembered his wide brimmed hat shading his face, tanned and bronzed from the sun. He was only forty-five years old when he was taken from his family and it would seem had too many years left to live for this to happen.

The fields included a tobacco allotment. James Carl's daddy took his last tobacco crop to Carthage to sell, but refused to accept "depression prices" and brought it back home and stored it in the barn where family and neighbors used it up over time. That was the year before his death took him from his family.

His mother sold hay from the barn, farm equipment, Old Jack, her big mule, and Dolly, a fine mare, to pay the costs involved in the funeral and burial plus medical bills, never letting a bill go past due. She was now alone with her seven children; her youngest son less than a year old, James Carl was only four, 3 more girls and 2 more sons. Her life was one of work and worry, but she never gave up on her aim to raise her children to have a future. Everyone in the family was energized by this foundation of hard work and stick-to-it attitude.

The family's life was completely changed. They planted a vegetable garden from seed bought with twenty dollars given from a local church. They did not have calves to kill for beef, just one cow for milk, but they did have a pig that was fattened with food scraps and slop to kill for pork. They planted fields of corn, green beans, tomatoes, and potatoes, all those things that could be canned and used for food in the winter. The six-room house had two fireplaces, and wood was cut to feed the fires to stay as warm as possible. Every room had a bed, maybe two, except the dining room and kitchen. Straight-backed chairs from the dining room were placed in a circle around the fireplace in the winter and moved to the coolness of the country porch in the summer.

That house with the embracing porches is still there today occupied by James Carl's oldest living sister. James Carl's daddy's carpentry has lasted for more than seventy years. Some additions have been added, but the basic building is still the same. In the front yard the box elder tree still stands.

The attached song, "Twin Coffins," describes the events of the death of father and grandmother within a day of one another because of a pneumonia epidemic raging through the countryside at that particular point in time.

Words and music for this song were written by James Carl Anderson, son and grandson of the loved ones placed in those twin coffins. Carl, as he is called, often presents this song at family gatherings and to senior citizens at assisted living facilities. He has earned a reputation in the community as a speaker, performer, and master of ceremonies.

When I reached the age of four, my dad walked me to the store.
He bought me food, candy, toys and much more.
During Christmas, grandma said, visit us and eat ginger bread.
So, mom and dad walked me to the old homestead.
Soon, pneumonia and the flu killed my dad and grandma, too.
Home-made coffins were made of poplar through and through.
A log truck hauled them to their graves.
Our family mourned for days and days.
Our mules were sold to pay the bills with no delays.
Life has never been the same since that epidemic came.
Only God knows what was to blame.
Life goes on day by day.

Where there is a will, there is a way.
So, why not make the most of life without delay?
When I turned seventy-five, the old box elder was still alive
That made the shade where my dad and grandma lay (laid).

MOONSHINE ISLAND

James Carl's first memory of "corn by the gallon" goes back to age three when he wore a pretty dress with little cats and balls engraved in the white and blue cloth which had been a feed sack. His mother wanted to make some jumpers for him, but he liked the little dress and wanted to keep wearing it. However, at four years old, his legs had to be covered in order to work in the tobacco field. He picked and killed big green worms that were on the tobacco leaves, getting stung and suffering the accompanying pain. Perhaps the hurt is what he remembers the most. During the tobacco season, the family had a special visitor, the High Sheriff of Jackson County, Tennessee. The sheriff and James Carl's father were very good friends. They talked in the living room for a few minutes and moved to the dining room for coffee. When his mother discovered they were spiking the coffee with moonshine, she ran them out of the house! She absolutely ordered the sheriff and her husband to "get out of her kitchen!" They did and in a hurry!

A few months later his father died from pneumonia. It was difficult for his mother to keep track of where all six children living in her home were all the time (one was in the Civilian Conservation Corps Camp in Georgia and two were deceased). Each year this four-year-old boy ventured farther away from the farm house which stood on Highway 56, five miles south of Gainesboro, Tennessee.

A log truck drove into the woods every day hauling "bug wood" to Double Springs to be picked up and carried away by a freight train. The truck was fascinating to watch as was a beautiful, yellow, single-engine airplane circling over the rural community. Day after day that yellow airplane circled closer and closer to the ground, but not one time did it

7

land in the level fields of the farm. James Carl figured it all out by the time he was eight years old. The truck was hauling something more important than "bug wood." Also, it occurred to him that the plane circled that area for a special reason. One day that truck sped out of the woods and turned upside down 100 yards from Highway 56 (Route 3). Men walked from the woods in a hurry. One man put two five-gallon buckets of slop (mash waste liquid – slop) on the back porch and came quickly into the house. The sheriff had found out where the corn was being converted into whiskey. A federal officer verified the location and the "flying feces hit the swirling blade." The big moonshine still located on a little island was cut to pieces. The whiskey was poured into a nearby stream. Some slop was carried away and fed to hogs. That pork was fed to poor hungry children.

A little island had been built where three farms met at their corners. No one, it seems, claimed the island and no one paid land taxes for it. It was a "no man's land." The employees escaped and no one was arrested. Apparently, the whiskey makers outsmarted the local sheriff and the U.S. Government officials.

Several men lost good paying jobs and the unemployment rate in Jackson County increased. Some of the skilled workers of Moonshine Island went to Detroit and helped build automobiles. Some went to California and worked in the oil fields. Some, who had fattened hogs on the slop, went to the Homesteads in Crossville, Tennessee, where they helped to create churches and guard German prisoners during World War II.

Those who refused to find more respectable jobs went over to another hollow two miles from Moonshine Island and continued their trade. They found short cuts which allowed them to make higher profits on pure corn whiskey. James Carl knew some of those men and was able to help two or three find jobs in Cookeville, Tennessee. Others continued to drink the "booze" and change corn and sugar into a profitable product. They made one major mistake. Instead of using a "copper worm" (a coiled condenser made of pure copper), they evidently used old automobile radiators. Some of these radiators had been repaired with lead solder. Some innocent people were poisoned when the lead combined with sulfates. Many people died with similar symptoms from 1940 to 1990. Could it have been lead poisoning as well as too much whiskey? Some of the victims were hard working people.

James Carl witnessed what crazy actions moonshine can cause men and women to take. One of his neighbors put his wife in the trunk of his 1935 Ford coupe and tried to knock down his father's new smoke house.

The driver broke planks on the homemade building and almost killed his wife! He bet $25 that his new 1935 Ford coupe could out pull Old Jack, the big mule. A big crowd met in the forest fifty yards north of his house on Highway 56 (Route 3), placed their bets, watched and listened. An argument followed. Would the car be on pavement? Would Old jack be on dirt? Well, Old Jack stood on firm ground. He was excited. His ears stood straight up. When his owner said "Getty up," the harness chains tightened. Old Jack jumped, planted his feet, and dragged that shiny black Ford coupe off Highway 56 across a drainage ditch and 100 feet into the forest. Old Jack was a proud mule. Those who won bets yelled and made a lot of noise. Some losers did not have the money to pay. Arguments led to pushing and shoving. Apparently the punch was spiked! It was a funny sight. A mule had out-pulled a V-8. Time helped to make things right. Some IOU notes were signed, the smoke house was repaired, and the drunk driver's wife lived to recover.

Moonshine Island faded into history with time. It is remembered only by a few senior citizens who lived near the moonshine still that prepared corn to be "sold by the gallon."

<u>TWO LAWMEN WHO ACTUALLY HELPED SOLVE THE</u> <u>"MOONSHINE" PROBLEM ON THE RIDGE</u>

Bill Mathis, pictured on the right, was one of the most effective lawman to serve in Jackson County, Tennessee, and on The Ridge. He played a key role in solving the "Moonshine" problem in the area.

Lewis Elkins, pictured on the left, was a close friend and lawman. He lost his life during a struggle with an outlaw.

HISTORIC HILLSIDE PLOW DISPLAYED ON THE RIDGE
AT THE ANDERSON FARM

The hillside plow shown above was actually used by
Tom Anderson, James Bedford, his son, and James
Bedford's sons, Herman, Fred, Carl and Clarence

SOME MODES OF TRANSPORTATION
ON THE RIDGE AND IN COOKEVILLE
IN THE LATE 19TH AND EARLY 20TH CENTURY

Mules, horses, buggies, wagons, and stage coaches were popular means of transportation on Avery Trace in the late 1700's. Steam-powered trains and gasoline-powered automobiles became popular modes of transportation in the early 20th century in the Cookeville area. Dr. McCoin owned one of the first Ford touring cars on The Ridge in the early 1900's.

SCHOOL IN NO MAN'S LAND

James Carl was four and one half years old when his father died from pneumonia. His mother was left with seven children and no income. Her oldest son was accepted in the CCC (a Civilian Conservation Corps Program established by President Franklin D. Roosevelt and the U.S. Congress). There were medical bills to pay for the treatment of the pneumonia, the devastating epidemic that swept the local populace, and his mother never let a bill go unpaid. She sold Jack, her big mule, Dolly, a very nice mare, farm implements, and hay from the barn loft to pay those medical bills.

An Elder from a local church came with a $20.00 offering to give to James Carl's mother. He overheard the Elder tell her, "This money is to buy garden seeds, not to buy food." They grew a beautiful garden that year and it provided fresh food for months. This experience taught the children a valuable lesson similar to the one learned at Plymouth Rock, Massachusetts, in 1620. "If we give you food you can eat today, but if we teach you how to catch fish and show you where they are, you can eat for many moons." The lesson is a good one today for those who depend on soup lines and bridges to cover the homeless. James Carl and his siblings learned early in life to grow food, can food, and conserve.

Every member of the family had to do their share to keep kith and kin together, clothed, and fed. Before walking to school every day, James Carl carried two buckets of fresh cold water from a big spring that was located down a steep hill three hundred yards away. One sister milked Roan, their cow, and fed a hog. Another sister helped his mother cook fresh farm eggs, plus a young fryer chicken, and make gravy from milk and flour. Another sister made up beds and swept floors. The oldest brother at home (14 years old) left very early in the morning to work at a nearby saw mill to earn money to pay for groceries and shoes to be worn only during the cold winter months. The youngest brother (4 years old) fed the chickens and gathered eggs. It was fascinating to watch his mother "ring" the head off the young fryer chicken before it was cooked. His mother was an excellent manager of the farm during those years when she alone was responsible for her seven living children. She lost two children as infants.

James Carl's first day of school was just prior to his sixth birthday. They walked one and three-tenths miles to and from school each day. Only those living at least two miles from school could ride the school bus. They made that trek back and forth every school day no matter the weather.

The teacher allowed his two older sisters to sit at a table with him that first day. After that, he became popular in the "Primer" class. The students had a year to learn to read before entering first grade. He learned to look at the pictures in the book, "Peter and Peggy," and report to the teacher what Peter and Peggy were doing. This caused the teacher to see him as a smart child. In addition, his mother or one of his sisters read each story to him a day prior to his next class. It actually took him a year to learn to read, but some of his classmates never learned to read or write.

Recess was fun. Children played marbles and caught June bugs. James Carl won the June bug contest. Each contestant caught a June bug, inserted a straw in its rear area, and turned it loose. His bug flew up, up, and out of sight, climbing the highest and flying the greatest distance. He won because he inserted the smallest straw!

Two students had an older brother as a teacher at the school. One day while taking a nap after his sack lunch, the teacher was rolled into a cold branch of water near the school building. Someone pushed him off that foot-log. No one knows if it was his younger brothers who did it, but these two brothers played some dandy Halloween tricks on The Ridge.

ANTIOCH SCHOOL ON FLYNN'S CREEK
(ORIGINAL BUILDING)

Members of the Anderson family attended and taught at this early school. This photo is dated about 1905. James Bedford Anderson (James Carl Anderson's father) is second from left in the front row. Next to him is James Chaffin. Johnny Anderson, teacher (brother to James Bedford) is on the back row, 4th from left. Effie Anderson, sister to Johnny and James Bedford, is in 3rd row from the back, 3rd from right. Next to her is Essie Chaffin, 2nd from right.

However, it was a very poor and extremely rural community. No one would claim the land across the road to avoid paying land tax. The wooden building had a "Little Room" (grades Primer through 4) and a "Big Room" (grades 5 through 8). Drinking water came from rain water off the roof and was stored in an underground tank. The outhouses were very unsanitary. Thirty to fifty students used them daily. There was no running water or toilet paper. Clean corn cobs were at a premium.

This rural school lost its certification in 1944. Its teacher failed to administer the state 8th grade examination. To go to high school a student was required to take and pass the eighth grade examination at a certified school. James Carl paid ten cents, rode the mail truck to Gainesboro, Tennessee, and took the test with those who were given a second chance. His score was among the very best in the county! The Superintendent wrote a special letter to the local high school principal and he became a freshman that year. Those who transferred to other schools from that little county school attended two or three years before being able to enter high school. He graduated high school with honors and was selected by a faculty of twenty-two teachers as the "Outstanding Student" in 1949.

At that rural county school, playing marbles was a big challenge. Big Caleb was sixteen years old and in third grade. He never did assignments and was always in trouble. When recess ended, the teacher rang a bell. While the students were playing the marble game of "keeps" and the bell rang, Big Caleb grabbed and kept all the marbles. One day six of them (ages 8-10) were playing and the bell rang. They had a plan that worked! They all attacked Big Caleb and took all of his marbles out of his pockets. The teacher went really easy on them for that ruckus. Big Caleb stopped stealing marbles from little boys. Big Caleb also stole food from James Carl's lunch pail almost every day. He caught him in the act. Big Caleb always took the half bar of Hershey candy. One day James Carl substituted "ExLax" for Hershey. Big Caleb enjoyed eating it, but failed to get to the outhouse in time. You see, they had to stand in line to go to the outhouse.

Big Caleb stopped stealing food, but ended up in big trouble. He was being corrected for fighting and turned on the teacher. He said, "Look out, Becky, I'm coming at you like a storm." As he passed by the potbelly coal stove, he threw a full box of 22-caliber bullets into the stove. The top cap flew off and the stove door flew open! The teacher ran to the "Big Room" to get help from the other teacher! Students jumped out windows, crowded the exit door, and generally panicked! The local school board expelled Big Caleb from school.

Big Caleb was not the oddest of all students at that school. Big Ben was, indeed, very unusual. His dad and mom brought him to his first day of school when he was nine years old. His mom had cut down a pair of his dad's Washington and Lee overalls for him to wear. Those overalls were very classy. They had a bib for pencils and pens, a loop to hold a hammer, big side and leg pockets and brass buttons and snaps. He was dressed to the hilt, even wearing shoes. A few weeks later the county sent a nurse to vaccinate students for Smallpox and other diseases. Big Ben kept going to the back of the line. When it was his turn, the nurse held a big, long needle up toward the ceiling and squirted a few drops of the ingredient and Big Ben ran to the nearest open window, jumped out, and ran home. That was his last day of school and he went through life uneducated.

The sons and daughters of parents who were employed at Moonshine Island wore shoes year round, were driven to school in shiny automobiles, and Santa Claus brought them new bicycles and leather holsters for their pearl-handled cap pistols. These "High Society" students were seldom whipped at the end of the school day for talking during class.

JAMES CARL ANDERSON IN ELEMENTARY SCHOOL

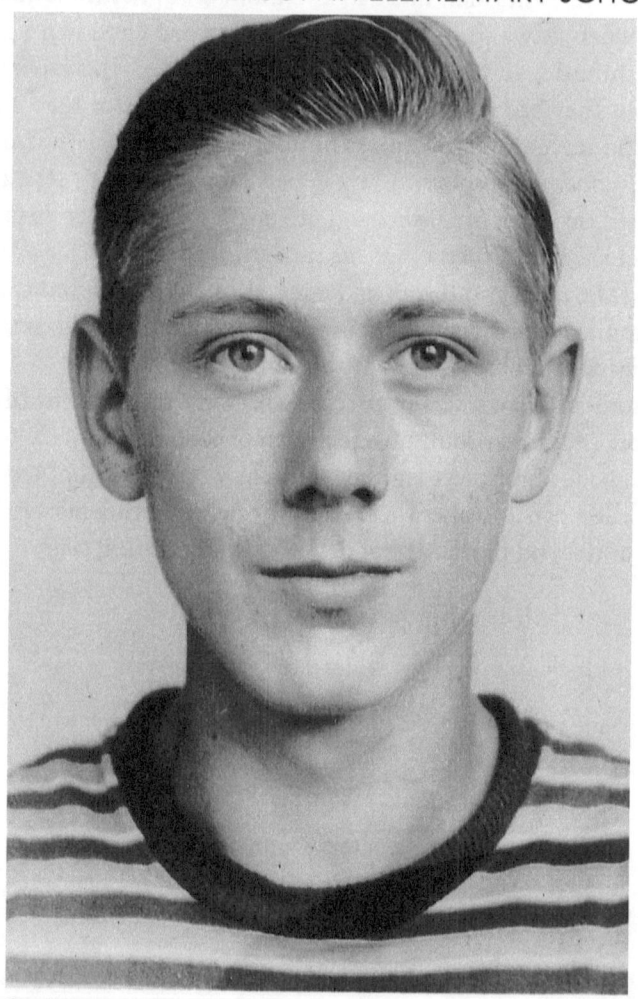

James Carl Anderson attended McCoinsville Elementary School in 1942 as a 12-year-old boy. The school implemented a hot lunch program and during a nine-month school term, James Carl gained 12 pounds, more than any other student. Miss Willie West was the teacher at that time doing an outstanding job.

Those who walked to and from school were often guarded by a special officer. This officer was operating in disguise and was actually one of the most sought after criminals in the U.S.! He was later arrested in Louisville, Kentucky, and died in the electric chair. That "deputy" was nice to children. Not only did he protect those who wore shoes, but he also helped barefooted children. One day he picked up James Carl and two other students in a downpour of rain and drove the three safely to school. His real name was discovered by local authorities a few days later and from that day forward, he was "on the run." He ran a red light in Louisville, Kentucky, and was chased by the local police. He tried to outrun the officer. Either he or his wife shot the officer and killed him. In the process he wrecked his car, jumped out and ran through a resident's yard, into the house and through the living room. The resident ran him down, wrestled him to the ground, and claimed a citizen's arrest. He held him until backup police arrived. This ordinary person had successfully apprehended one of the nation's most wanted criminals, an escaped prisoner from a Wisconsin prison. Those students were guarded by a celebrity, but did not realize it until they read about him in the local newspaper.

James Carl learned early on that a little fellow had to be smart and intelligent to be popular at that little rural school. A small, 90-pound boy could not out do a 160-pound, 16-year-old redneck. James Carl was inspired to stay up an extra hour at night to do all his homework and then some. After he learned the nine numbers of arithmetic, he added the letters and symbols to advance to algebra and geometry. He read Macbeth and Julius Caesar at home. The teacher promoted him two grade levels in one year. He helped Big Caleb with his arithmetic and Big Caleb taught him to play marbles, volley ball, and shoot a sling shot. Big Caleb could whistle, make a snake stick its head upward three inches and cut its head off with a steel ball (steel ball from a Ford Model-T wheel bearing) from his slingshot. The rubber strings came from old Model-T inner tubes. He could wind up and do a 360-degree slam dunk over the volley ball net while his body was still in the air. He taught James Carl to set the volleyball in place for the slam dunk. Even at 90 pounds, James Carl played on an undefeated team in his fifth grade year.

World War II was getting into full swing. Two of James Carl's teammates (seventeen years old) became heroes in the U.S. Army, entering after that school year. Twenty-five years later, James Carl reviewed the careers of twenty-five former school mates. Some of those students excelled. One performed heroically as a Captain in the U.S. Air Force. Three school mates were heroes in World War II; one was shot out of the sky as a Navigator.

After the war ended, one former school mate married the Assistant Librarian at a State University, finished his Masters Degree, and became an Assistant Librarian. Another was on two undefeated athletic teams, earned three university degrees, served 40 professional years in education and was listed in "Who's Who in America." Last but not least, two of these fifth grade classmates played on a Livingston Academy basketball team that won forty-four consecutive basketball games. These two also excelled in academics at James Carl's elementary school and Gainesboro Elementary School.

That wooden school building burned soon after James Carl's class finished the eighth grade. Most of the families associated with the school attended church services there at one o'clock on Sunday afternoons. After the building burned, they met under a big pine tree on the campus. They threw dollar bills instead of dimes and quarters in the hat on Sundays and built a nice brick building in 1953, which is one of the most successful congregations in the county today. These were "salt of the earth" people. Former employees of Moonshine Island are today pillars of the community. They manage local stores, garages, small businesses, and farms and hold political offices. Corn is now used for bread. Licensed liquor stores operate and provide tax money to build school buildings. The buildings have sanitary bathrooms. This memory describes one of the biggest "turn around" educational projects, ever, in Tennessee.

JACKSON COUNTY CENTRAL HIGH SCHOOL BUILDING
FLAG POLE WAS ERECTED DECEMBER 6, 1941

Several young men and women from Jackson County
Central High School volunteered for military service after
the Japanese bombed Pearl Harbor on December 7,
1941. World War II proved that freedom is not cheap.

SPYING FOR GENERAL PATTON

December 7, 1941, was a very cold winter day in Jackson County, Tennessee. A neighbor woman came running down the road screaming at the top of her voice, "The Japs have bombed us." "Yes, the Japs have bombed us." James Carl was only a ten-year-old boy and asked, "Is anyone hurt?" She said, "Yea, they sank our ships and killed our sailors." He asked, "Where?" She said, "Out in the ocean in a pearl harbor."

In 1941 there was no electricity on Route 3, Gainesboro, Tennessee, but the woman had an old RCA radio hooked up to a car battery. So she had some very accurate news. She even said that President Roosevelt and Secretary of State Cordell Hull were very mad at the Japs. Cordell Hull, a devout man, was heard cursing the Japs and their leader, Tojo. That car battery-powered RCA radio said that Roosevelt and Hull may ask the U.S. Congress to declare war on the Japs.

The neighbor woman's brother rigged up a water wheel (made from a bicycle wheel) and connected it to an old Ford Model-A generator. He recharged the battery and hooked up the radio the next day. The radio announced over WHUB in Cookeville, Tennessee, "The U.S. has declared war on Japan."

One of the more educated women in this little rural farm community said, "This is clairvoyance." James Carl asked, "What does that mean?" To teach James Carl she explained that our brand new high school put up a new flag pole on December 6; the Japs bombed Pearl Harbor on December 7; and several of the local high school seniors volunteered the very next day to fight the Japs. The local high school football team had gone undefeated and untied. These fine athletes were drafted at the end of the school year.

James Carl's big brother worked for Ford Motor Company in Detroit,

Michigan. He had bought a new Ford V-8 a few months before and had promised to teach James Carl to drive, so he was anxious for his brother to drive down to Tennessee. He did, and while James Carl was learning to shift gears and drive the almost new Ford, he explained that he would soon be going into the U.S. Army for basic training. He entered the U.S. Army in February, 1942. After completing basic training, he attended a medical training program at Fort Sam Houston, Texas, and probably thought he would be fighting Japanese. While he was being trained, German submarines sank some U.S. ships in the Atlantic Ocean. The U.S. declared war on Germany. The dictator, Adolph Hitler, had trained a good army, navy and air force. Pictures of his army tanks and fighter planes were in fifth grade school books. The U.S. was in for a bloody war. James Carl was eleven years old when his brother was shipped across the Atlantic Ocean to North Africa.

He once explained to James Carl that the first few hours were quiet near Casablanca, North Africa. His first casualty was a little black African boy hiding behind a little shack. As James Carl's brother threw a can of K rations toward the building to crash the can of beans open, the little boy peeped his head out in the path of the beans. The can hit the boy exactly between the eyes. The boy almost died, but luckily survived after some stitches and medication.

The German tanks, half tracks, cannons, fighter planes and foot soldiers arrived the next day. One old country boy described it as, "All Hell broke loose." The Germans proved to be well-disciplined soldiers. However, the Americans, with sheer force and numbers, pushed the Germans and some of their best generals back across the sands of North Africa. Perhaps the most feared German shell those first days of land war was an "88." After the war ended, James Carl's brother explained that while driving a mail jeep, an "88" blew a huge crater directly in front of his jeep. The last thing he remembered for many days was his jeep flipping end over end as he and the jeep plunged into the huge hole. Shrapnel from the shell scarred his arms and back for life. He was flown to England in a C-47 and luckily recovered in time to be in on the Sicily invasion.

By this time James Carl had reached the age of twelve and his thought was that in five years he would be old enough to go over there and help his brother. He saw an Army jeep climb the county courthouse steps every time someone bought a U.S. War Bond. A decorated U.S. Army Colonel arrived in Gainesboro and was admired by local politicians and business men. His name was Patton. He took some local people for rides to different communities in the area. He encouraged brave young men and women to enter the fight against Hitler, the mean dictator. He was a big hit in Jackson County and pledged to bring his troops here and train to whip Hitler.

James Carl lived on a rural farm five miles south of Gainesboro. Each weekday morning at 2:00 A.M. he heard the choo-choo train (huge freight train) blow its whistle several times as it topped Buffalo Valley Mountain. However, one cold damp morning he could not hear the train. There was a loud roaring noise from the East. The noise got louder and louder. The noise continued for thirty minutes, then an hour, and finally lights appeared. Jeeps arrived; trucks arrived, followed by half tracks and last, but not least, heavily armored tanks. Hundreds and, perhaps, thousands of soldiers and vehicles passed by the farm house on Highway 56 South (Route 3, Gainesboro, Tennessee). General Patton and his First Army had arrived to train to whip Hitler.

Even before Patton's troops arrived for training, James Carl started his own training. He gave up the sling shot and mastered an air rifle. Next, a neighbor woman trained him to adjust the aim and shoot a real rifle. They tied an ear of corn to the top of a fence post 100 yards away and waited for the next crow. She finally killed a crow at that distance. General Patton's soldiers were very impressed. Some of the soldiers tried and missed. When James Carl mastered the 22 rifle at that distance, he felt real good about himself. Thanks to that lady who cut his hair, taught him to do fractions, and shoot a rifle.

Patton's First Army was divided into two equal-size armies for maneuvers. Referees were assigned. Actually it was a war game with specific rules. Patton's Army (red, white and blue) represented the U.S. Army. James Carl said to himself, "I'll help this side against the Germans." He did. He also recruited a squad to help. They built a tree house as an observation post. They spied on the enemy and reported to Patton's side. They actually designed and built wire communications to machine-gun posts and gave friendly troops advance warning. They provided cold well water and hot fresh food (against the rules, but they did it as spies.).

There was Joe Nathan Johnson, age 10, Charles Johnson, age 10, Clarence Anderson, age 8, and James Carl Anderson had reached the age of 13. These boys did not know that they were spies, but James Carl knew. Charles and James Carl, with the help of Charles' dad, repaired a 1942 Army Dodge truck that had double dual wheels and ten-wheel drive. The truck's mission for General Patton was crucial for the order of the day. They took a six-volt coil off a wrecked Model-A Ford and installed it on top of the six-cylinder Dodge engine. The truck engine started, and the truck and an entire platoon of armed soldiers completed a secret mission against so-called enemy troops.

When General Patton was questioned by the referees about using civilians in the battles he had won, he replied, "When I get there, I'll do it to the Germans too." He did, and how, thanks to him! Apparently, General Patton's troops were so impressed with what some children had done to help win the battle games that real Army tents, canteens, some clothes and even rations were issued to the Spy Squad for camping.

JAMES CARL ANDERSON SCHOOL DAYS

School Days

James Carl Anderson wanted very much to own a real leather jacket when he was a young boy. He worked at Vestel Johnson's sawmill after completing his eighth grade school year (Summer of 1945) providing cold spring drinking water for eight sawmill workers, moving sawdust away from the belts and pulleys (dust monkey), and helping Vestel haul firewood made from "slabs." He earned $1.00 for each eight-hour work day. He paid $16.99 for his new leather jacket from a Sears Roebuck Catalogue. He was a popular freshman at Jackson County Central High School in his leather zip-up jacket. He also bought a pair of real leather shoes!

James Carl's brother recovered from the wounds he received in North Africa, and participated in the invasion of Sicily and Italy. He was again seriously wounded and returned to England to recover in time for the invasion of France at Normandy. Luckily, he survived some very close calls at Normandy; however, he enjoyed a few days in Paris, France, before facing a good German Army in retreat across France. It would seem the U.S. forces advanced a bit too hastily and were surrounded while marching toward Germany. James Carl's brother was captured by the Germans on September 3, 1944. Thousands of his fellow soldiers were surrounded by Hitler's Army. The U.S. Army was running out of ammunition, food, and time during a frigid cold winter at the Battle of the Bulge. General Patton and the Army that trained in the region around Gainesboro, Tennessee, came to the rescue! Against all odds, General Patton told his command staff that, if allowed to do so, his men could move 100 miles on foot, through snow and ice, in time to whip the Germans and free the trapped U. S. troops. He did!

The U.S. Army and Air Force crossed the Rhine River, whipped the Germans, and rescued James Carl's brother and many other prisoners of war from "Stalag 12-A" and Jewish citizens from gas chambers. General Patton and his troops utilized many of the tactics they learned in Tennessee, especially calling on civilians to obtain gasoline, food, and drinking water as they suffered, traveling 100 miles over terrain they were advised it was impossible to cover. Patton convinced his men that they could do it and they did. To the surprise of his superiors, his Army broke the deadlock at the Battle of the Bulge and sent the German Army in a near stampede to its mainland. Hitler and some of his top Generals committed suicide and the Allied Forces won World War II in Europe and, a few months later, in the South Pacific three days after the first Atomic Bomb was dropped on Hiroshima, Japan.

After James Carl's brother returned to Vanderbilt hospital for several weeks of treatment due to outside weather exposure, malnutrition, and serious wounds, he and other World War II veterans would meet for target practice. One day they chose a specific rooster to be the target. A rule was established that they would aim only at its head. After an entire box of 22-caliber bullets were shot at the rooster's head, he jumped up on a concrete wall fifty yards away and crowed as if to say, "I won." To the surprise of all those World War II veterans, James Carl took a lone 22-caliber bullet, put it in a borrowed rifle, and shot the rooster in the eye. They ate that rooster for dinner.

Apparently, Sergeant Alvin C. York heard of this feat and he visited James Carl at the Atlas Boot Company in Cookeville. He said the U.S. was entering a "Cold War" with the Soviet Union, and he offered to recommend James Carl to study Rural Officer Training Corps (ROTC) at Tennessee Tech University. James Carl accepted his recommendation, and, four years later, became a Second Lieutenant in the U.S. Army Signal Corps. When James Carl went on the firing range at Fort Carson, Colorado, in 1955, he was one of the very few of 20,000 soldiers to hit all six bulls eyes, at a distance of 300 yards while in the standing position. The Expert Rifle Medal was awarded.

James Carl was too young to put on a uniform and help free his brother from a POW camp during World War II. He went on active duty as an officer after the truce was signed between South and North Korea. He completed his tour of active and reserve duty before the Vietnam War started. So, he did not shoot Germans, North Koreans, or Vietnamese.

Also, he was not shot at by a military enemy. However, while walking from elementary school, he was shot by accident. A poor neighboring family was without food and sent three sons to kill a rabbit or squirrel. Their rabbit hounds were chasing a jack rabbit across a hill top. Just as the rabbit came into clear view at 10:00, two shot guns, aimed at the rabbit "let go" BANG/BANG. Charles Johnson was on James Carl's left. Clarence, his younger brother was on his right. A highway bank (Old Highway 56 in Jackson County) protected their legs and feet.

Charles Johnson took some dozen buck shots in his left side through a leather coat, shirt, heavy underwear and two layers of tissue. James Carl took in about six buck shots. Clarence was protected by the other two on his left side. The concussion and pressure of those buck shots forced them two feet toward the middle of the highway. They survived. The jack rabbit was killed. The hunters apologized. Charles' parents never allowed him to walk to school (1.3 miles) again. So, James Carl was shot, but not in war.

In this chapter, James Carl's brother was Herman C. Anderson, born in 1917. He was James Carl's "big brother" and a good one. He taught James Carl to drive his new Ford, box with gloves, and follow the rules. It was not the army that taught James Carl how to shoot a rifle. The neighbor woman who cut his hair at age five and six, helped him with fractions in arithmetic, and taught him how to adjust the aim and shoot a rifle accurately, paved the way for him to succeed in marksmanship. Her name was Mary Johnson, Vestal Johnson's wife. Vestal gave James Carl a sawmill job (dust monkey) to pay his way through high school. Vestal recommended him to work at General Motors in Detroit, Michigan, to help pay his way through Tennessee Tech.

Sergeant York not only helped James Carl to become a U.S. Army Officer. He, in addition, sent him to an institution of higher learning. Although, James Carl never knew General Patton personally, his First Army gave him some very good training in communications which, without doubt, helped him to become a U.S. Army Signal Corps Officer. A Top Secret security clearance helped him to achieve some pretty sophisticated training for soldiers who served during the Vietnam War. He, still today, is glad he served.

FIRST LIEUTENANT JAMES CARL ANDERSON SERVED IN THE U.S. ARMY SIGNAL CORPS DURING THE KOREAN WAR ERA

Sgt Alvin C. York recommended James Carl Anderson to study Military Science (R.O.T.C.) at Tennessee Tech during the Korean War. Anderson served with the Fifth Army's 529th Signal Company and helped to develop and test some state-of-the-art radio and wire communications equipment.

POVERTY ON THE RIDGE

When James Carl reached the age of twelve, he was the oldest male in the family at home. His father had died with pneumonia when he was four years old. Herman, his oldest brother, was in the U.S. Army Medical Corps during World War II. Fred, an older brother, lived in Detroit, Michigan. His mother was stuck with two daughters and two sons, all in elementary school, and no one old enough to get a job. Times were tough and food was scarce. His mother took hand-me-down overalls, used her pedal-powered Singer sewing machine and made James Carl jumpers. He went bare foot most of the year, even to school.

A local church elder brought his mother $20.00 and told her, "This money is to buy garden seeds......not groceries." They made a garden, with hand and hoe, and canned food for the winter months. James Carl remembered the teaching he had learned in school that Indians told the settlers at Plymouth Rock, Massachusetts, in 1620, "We can give you food for a day, but if we show you how to catch fish and tell you where to find the fish, you can eat for many moons."

An old time farmer, who felt sorry for the family's situation, came to the house, talked to his mother and offered him a job. He paid James Carl 10 cents an hour to hoe corn with his son on a new ground hillside. After five work days, he handed James Carl $3.00. James Carl sat the old man down and explained that "sun-up to sun-down" was about twelve hours, and the pay should be $6.00. He asked, "How'd you know that?" James Carl showed him how to multiply 10 cents and twelve hours and then multiply by five days. The old man never stopped thanking James Carl for showing him how to do simple arithmetic on paper! He then showed his sixteen-year-old son, Big Ben, how to do it.

After two weeks, James Carl had saved up $12.00, enough money to attend the Friday night carnival in Gainesboro. His older brother, Fred, was home on vacation from Detroit and they went together. They went to the naked woman show. All her singing, dancing, twisting, and teasing did not impress James Carl enough for him to pay 30 cents (3 hours of hard work). He chose to spend his next three dimes trying to win a beautiful big carnival ware bowl. He lost 30 cents without winning a thing, but came very close. He tried again. After spending fifty cents (5 hours of hard work), he won the prettiest bowl on display, and took it home.

While not working on Saturday, he practiced how to throw a dime into a carnival bowl from a distance of ten feet. After about 100 tries, he was able to bounce the dime from the side of the bowl straight up in the air and back to the bottom of the bowl. He spent $3.00 (30 hours of labor), but he won six big carnival ware bowls. People were standing in line to pay $2.00 each for those six bowls. After eating a hamburger and drinking a Pepsi, he returned to make another easy $12.00. After he won four more bowls, the game manager told him that he had won the limit. A deputy sheriff was standing by watching and said, "There's no limit."

The game manager packed up and went home. James Carl bought a new pair of good leather shoes and some Washington and Lee overalls for school. Thirty years later he sold two of those carnival ware bowls at a yard sale for $16.00 each and bought a nice pair of Botany 500 pants!

When neighbor boys heard of the corn hoeing and business success, they visited and tried to show off. One Saturday, they challenged James Carl to play Follow the Leader. When it was his time to be the leader, he chose tree climbing as his specialty. His feet were very tough on the bottom from all the bare foot walking and his hands were very strong from all the corn hoeing. He picked out a tall, young hickory tree with very few limbs. He climbed up almost 20 feet, and held tight with both hands and jumped outward, taking the tree down to within two feet of the ground and letting go. It looked easy. It also looked like fun. Oliver tried it. He climbed to the same height and yelled, "I knew I could do it." He held on, jumped outward. The hickory tree bent a little bit, but there he hung 16 feet above the ground (two stories above ground). He yelled, "Help!!" You see, Oliver only weighed 60 pounds. James Carl weighed 110 pounds. He held on. The boys quickly piled up some hickory and oak leaves. He fell fifteen feet and landed safely in a bed of leaves.

When Big Caleb, the former student who told teacher Miss Becky to "Stand by, I'm coming through like a storm" (He threw a box of 22 caliber shells in a pot bellied coal stove.), challenged James Carl to be the leader, he chose "riding in the truck tire." He had done it many times and taught his little brother to lean to right and turn right and to lean left and go left. However, no one had taught big, rough and tough Big Caleb to guide the big truck tire. He sat in the tire, and they started it rolling toward the saw dust pile on a hillside. They told him, "Now guide it on the road, over the sawdust pile and between the big trees." "No problem," he yelled as they let go. The road was straight at first and he made it to the sawdust pile. He gained speed, lost sense of where he was, failed to turn (did not know to lean left or right), and collided straight on with the biggest oak tree on the hillside! The tire bent together with him sitting in it. The tire and Big Caleb went in opposite directions for ten feet. Big Caleb lay flat on the ground and turned white, not moving, not speaking. All the follow-the-leaders thought he was dead. His mom was attending a funeral a half mile from the dreadful scene. James Carl ran to tell her and get medical help. When they returned to the accident spot, Big Caleb had come to and was eating blackberries off some nearby briars. Everybody thanked goodness that he was alive.

Now six weeks had passed since James Carl and Big Ben had planted that huge hillside of new ground corn. The plants were perhaps the best on The Ridge. Three acres were expected to produce about 200 bushels of corn. At $1.50 a bushel, Big Ben would be rich. James Carl showed Big Ben how to multiple $1.50 by 200 because it would take too much time to add $1.50 200 times. Big Ben thought he was a genius. If Big Ben had not jumped out the window and went home the day the smallpox nurse squirted medicine in the air from a big, long needle, he, too, could have figured his future wealth ($300).

After James Carl told Big Ben of his luck at the local carnival, he decided to make more than $300 on his corn. Seven weeks after they had planted the corn, he gathered a bushel of green corn and sold it for ten cents an ear and asked each family to save the cobs for him. He figured out how to get $3.00 for each bushel of green corn and dry cobs from corn on the cob. Cobs were worth money when out houses were common on The Ridge. A good dry cob sold for one cent. Big Ben sold half of his corn crop when it was green. After he gathered his corn for meal and corn bread, he cut off the corn leaves (fodder) and fed his old mule during the winter. His corn crop helped him put $400 in the bib of his Washington and Lee overalls. He then bought new shirts and shoes.

If the still on Moonshine Island had not been cut down by the Federal folks, Big Ben's corn might have sold "by the gallon." Who knows?

He might have realized $500 or $600 for his corn. Moonshine Island was within yelling distance upstream from the new ground corn field. Big Ben's corn money sure came in handy. His mother died during child birth, and he was able to buy some real nice planks and cloth to make her a decent coffin. He even had money to pay the preacher. The newborn boy survived and lived to eat cornbread from Big Ben's corn crop.

In the meantime, Big Caleb's father apparently went crazy. After fathering 20 children, the burden of family life overwhelmed him. He did not own a hillside of new ground to grow corn. He lost his tobacco base. One son was in jail for stealing frying chickens from a nearby store. His oldest son was burned beyond recognition at The Battle of the Bulge. His daughter and two grand children had died in a recent flood. A younger son was injured in the riots of Bell Isle in Detroit. When his remaining family (12 of them) was literally starving to death, he killed his mule, and it fed them for several days. He was placed in an asylum in Nashville and died there.

Within days, Big Ben's father met Big Caleb's mom at a Cake Walk and Liar's Contest at the same old building where Big Caleb blew up the pot-bellied stove. Big Ben had money to win a cake. He and a local school girl ate it.

The Liar's Contest stole the show. Oscar told of working on Sgt. York's water-powered grist mill in Jamestown, Tennessee, and said, "I adjusted the water spout and it turned the water wheel backwards; then it un-ground two bushels of corn before I could stop it. Big Ben's dad thought of telling the truth about his son's corn business, but did not. He was too busy flirting with Big Caleb's mom. He also won her a cake.

A poor backwoods man stood up and said, "I am so poor that I always run up beside a rabbit, and feel of its ribs before I shoot it; I don't like to waste 22 caliber bullets." He won second place. The first place winner was Charlie. He was known as the biggest liar from one end of The Ridge to the other. He even lied under oath and spent time in the pen. Old Charlie stood up and said four words ....."I have never lied." Charlie won first place in the lying contest.

Big Ben's father and Big Caleb's mom were married the next day by a Justice of The Peace. Their two combined families featured 27 children.

Some neighbors rumored that she was "too much for him." He died shortly thereafter. Luckily, he and Big Ben, his son, had grown some corn and tobacco. They sent some tax money to Nashville and made her eligible for Social Security. She moved to Nashville and boasted, "I can still throw a cat up on the roof." She married a third husband, listened to much good country and bluegrass music, and saw many beautiful sunsets behind the tall buildings of Nashville during her retirement years.

Big Ben continued to grow corn and tobacco and became an outstanding crosscut saw operator. He also made good money selling fox and mink furs. Members of both families sent good workers to the post World War II factories in Cookeville and Gainesboro. These "salt of the earth" families helped to replace buggies and wagons on The Ridge with cars and trucks. The younger siblings learned to sing, clog, and square dance. In brief, they adjusted socially on The Ridge. They played a key role in building a nice brick church building. Today, it has the most active members of any church in the entire county. Some of the pillars of the community still live on The Ridge.

Different people had different ways of earning money during those hard times. One local man earned money boxing up North for as much as $500 a fight. He challenged James Carl to a fight on a Sunday afternoon in the front yard of the family home near the box elder tree. Not one to run away from an attempt to belittle him, James Carl accepted and the fight was on. What the challenger did not know was that James Carl had won 13 bouts in gloves competition. A big crowd gathered even though most thought it would be a mismatch, a seasoned 50-year old boxer against a much younger boy. James Carl's corn hoeing had made his arms and fists strong and his feet firm. In his tall, lean frame, he had the ability to outmaneuver his larger opponent and take him down. It was a hard fight, but James Carl won. Boys on The Ridge stopped pushing him around. The two are friends still today.

The same year, Uncle Henry Johnson, a Blacksmith just across the road (Highway 56) was making horse shoes from Ford Model-T axles. Butch Allen, a teenager who went barefoot most of the year, walked up very close to Uncle Henry. Butch's feet were leather tough on the bottom. Butch stepped on a red-hot piece of metal that Uncle Henry had thrown on the ground. Uncle Henry said, "Butch, you stepped on a hot piece of metal." Butch said, "Which foot?"

The little fellow who could not ride the tall, slim Hickory tree to the ground survived the 20-foot fall and later became a Captain in the U.S.

Military. Also, three members of his Ridge Runner Baseball Team became commissioned officers during the Korean War era. To this day, people are still asking, "How in this world did those boys from The Ridge become prominent military leaders during the 50-year Cold War?" Perhaps, they applied themselves academically, physically and mentally. Their lives were put in harm's way to preserve freedom and democracy. With the help of God and a bit of luck, they survived.

JAMES CARL ANDERSON'S FATHER,
JAMES BEDFORD ANDERSON,

WITH HIS FRIEND, DR. McCOIN, SECOND FROM LEFT,

MRS McCOIN, AND TOM, THEIR LITTLE SON

Good friends enjoy watermelon while they discuss how to
purchase, service, and maintain one of the very first Ford
Model-T's on The Ridge(seen in the background), about 1910.

Oliver Anderson of Peter's Hollow and Robert Anderson (Bob) of The Ridge, pose in typical attire of successful young adults off the farm in the 1920's. They worked in Detroit, Michigan, long enough to buy new cars and some farm land and date successful young ladies.

JEALOUSY ON THE RIDGE

When early Colonists sent their folks westward into Tennessee Territory, some of the Anderson, Birdwell, Loftis, Hale, Jackson, Locke, Fox, Flatt, Jones, Johnson, Davis, Pharris, and Cantrell families got off the wagon trains near Flynn's Creek. The first East Tennessee to Middle Tennessee road was named Avery Trace. The state road was built adjacent to Flynn's Creek for many miles. There were times when the road was actually in the creek bed. Andrew Jackson, a young attorney and future President of the United States (U.S.), decided to travel past the present day Antioch community and Fort Blount to present day Nashville and the Hermitage. One of the very early schools near Flynn's Creek and Avery Trace was Antioch. James Carl's grandfather, grandmother, father and mother attended school there. Many of his cousins excelled in academics at Antioch before attending high schools and universities. Two of these cousins were Omer Hale and Edward D. Birdwell. They were a few years older than James Carl and probably felt sorry for him....their cousin from a poverty-stricken family. However, they did respect him because his volleyball team had gone undefeated during his fifth grade year. James Carl's school was McCoinsville Elementary School on The Ridge near "No Man's Land."

His cousins had excelled at Antioch in academics, not volleyball. They had some good rabbit hounds and they invited him to go rabbit hunting with them on his 12th birthday. Actually, James Carl thought they wanted to show him up. He did not have a gun, but he did have a good sling-shot.

They bragged about how good they were in high school algebra and geometry and he was still struggling with fractions, decimals, and early American History at McCoinsville. They could not wait to show James

41

Carl what good riflemen they were. Each cousin had a nice 22-caliber rifle and a box of bullets. Finally, their rabbit hounds picked up a rabbit scent and followed it. The hounds ran in a big circle and came past them about 50 feet away.…..and, lo and behold, there went the rabbit. Bang, bang, two rifles sounded off, and the rabbit went left and right and did a tight circle and the hounds lost its trail for a spell. Apparently, the rabbit got tired of waiting and "popped up" very close to the rabbit hounds and rapidly took off straight ahead. While the hounds smelled the ground, the rabbit increased its distance from the hounds and, possibly, could have escaped. Why, no one knows, but the rabbit played cat and mouse and started another big circle….bang, bang, and the rabbit completed its big circle. Those cousins might have had more luck with semi-automatic or automatic rifles, but one shot each time was not enough. The rabbit hounds showed less interest the third time around. By this time, James Carl had outguessed the rabbit and positioned himself near its big circle. He put a steel ball in his sling-shot, pulled back the rubber bands, and waited. When the rabbit approached, it saw him and almost stopped. He let go and wham! The steel ball sent the rabbit tumbling, but did not kill it. Before the hounds caught up, the rabbit, in pain, hid in a nearby hollow log.

The feat with the sling-shot gained James Carl some respect. His two cousins and the two rabbit hounds tried for an hour to get the rabbit out of the hollow log. All of their geometry and algebra did not help them solve the problem. The hounds' ability to smell did not solve the problem. James Carl wanted to eat that rabbit and did not give up. He suggested that one of them walk across the road and get their dad's axe and sledge hammer. His experience, while working at a sawmill, helped him figure out how to solve the problem. An ax was needed. They had polk sallet that was picked off that hillside and stewed rabbit for his 12th birthday dinner.

Omer and Edward D. were embarrassed. They were not as good with rifles as they thought. Their skills in mathematics did not help them get the rabbit out of the hollow log. They were determined to show off to their much younger cousin who had worked at a sawmill. They decided to assign James Carl an impossible task.

They took the rabbit to the house and asked Aunt Eva to cook it. Next, Omer was thrilled to show off the "Truckles" he had built. His invention featured big wheels that he and Willie, his dad, had cut from a big hickory tree. They drilled holes in the center, and mounted each wheel on a wooden axle. The frame was made of 2x4 oak lumber. The front axle could be turned left and right. A junked bicycle seat had been mounted in the very center of this gravity-powered vehicle.

The truckles had a six-foot long rope tied to each end of the front axle. James Carl's cousins had pulled each other around the barn and over the level yard when they were much younger. The wooden home-made wagon had been outside through several cold winters and had soaked up water from a hundred soaking rains so it was nowhere as strong as it once had been. They gave James Carl the honor of testing it over a steep hill. The path led down to a fresh-water spring where Omer had carried two big buckets of water to the house two times a day. They said that it should be a smooth ride until he came to a 90-degree turn near the spring. James Carl was a good fifth grader, but he did not know what ninety degrees meant. He had not been taught geometry or how to read a compass, but he was anxious to ride.

They stood beside the path 50 yards down the hill. James Carl made a turn to the right and one to the left and waved at them just before he headed down the steep straight away. That gravity-powered wagon picked up speed, lots of speed, and straight ahead was the 90 degree curve coming at him. There was a fifteen foot dropoff straight down. He had to try going around that steep curve. He almost made it, but a big rock in the road changed his course. The truckles bounced, went into a slide, out of control. It was a smooth ride through the air until the wagon collided with a big red beech tree. James Carl leaned left and got past the tree through the air several feet down the steep hill. The next thing he remembered was cold water in his face. The cousins dragged him several feet to the cold stream of water from the spring. They smiled when they thought that they had brought him back to life. Both front wheels were broken to pieces. The main frame and front axle were broken in half. The pieces were left to rot within yelling distance of Moonshine Island.

James Carl limped with his cousins up the steep hill and back to Omer's home. Eva, his second cousin, put Watkins salve on his wounds and patched him up before they enjoyed his birthday dinner of polk sallet and stewed rabbit.

Omer graduated from high school with honors that year and was drafted into the U.S. Army. He was taught to shoot a rifle correctly and throw hand grenades. He also was taught to use his geometry skills to aim artillery shells at German tanks and other big targets. His geometry came in handy when his entire outfit was surrounded by a good German Army at the Battle of the Bulge in 1944. He and his buddies held out until General Patton (He trained his Army in Middle Tennessee in 1942) moved his men more than 100 miles through winter snow, mud and debris, broke the German lines and rescued thousands of cold, hungry, and sleepy American Soldiers.

After World War II ended in 1945, Omer told me that the "end was near" when General Patton arrived and rescued an entire Army. Only hours before Patton's arrival, one of Omer's friends was directing military traffic at a muddy crossing. As he pointed for the tank to turn, he realized it was a German Panzer. He hit the ditch and survived. A bazooka destroyed the enemy tank. Omer became a proud U.S. Army veteran, retired as a leading executive of a good company, and enjoyed a respectable family life in Tennessee.

Edward D. graduated just as World War II ended. He was drafted, but was not shot at by Germans or Japanese. He also learned to shoot a rifle. He was a proud American Soldier. After receiving an honorable discharge, he worked at U.S. Rubber Tire Company on East Jefferson Street in Detroit, Michigan. He and James Carl attended Tennessee Tech together. He was James Carl's mentor for a summer. He drove him to Detroit where James Carl found employment to finish his Bachelor of Science Degree. Edward D. retired from U.S. Rubber and sold Bibles. He was an Elder in his church in Detroit, Michigan. Prior to his untimely death from a heart attack, Edward D. spent his annual vacations with his family on The Ridge.

That 12th year birthday party of hunting rabbits, riding a gravity-powered wagon, and eating stewed rabbit and polk sallet led to lifelong friendships and respect. Also, closer ties were made between the Antioch community on Flynn's Creek and the McCoinsville community on The Ridge. Jealousies among some cousins disappeared.

BIG MEETING ON THE RIDGE

When both James Carl's parents were living, his father and mother rode in the green seat of their new John Deer farm wagon, pulled by a pair of twin mules, Jack and John, each Sunday to Church at Antioch. Church was held in the old school building where his mom and dad attended school in the 1890's and early 1900's. They were married in the same old school building during a church wedding.

"Uncle Biss," James Carl's early mentor, lived in the Antioch community. He knew James Carl's mom and dad from the time they were born. In fact, he was born in about 1850, and knew his grandfather very well. "Uncle Biss" told about the Yankee soldiers visiting his home during their march to Stone's River Battle during the Civil War in the 1860's. They took his dad's horses with them. A few weeks later, the Rebel soldiers visited his home and took his dad's cow and several hogs for milk and meat. Believe it or not, a few days later, a "rag-tag" group of men came by and took the potatoes, apples and hickory-cured ham out of their underground cellar! As it turned out, the rag-tag bunch of no-good fellows were not soldiers of either side. They were trying to chase widows and young women all the way from Nashville to Knoxville.

"Uncle Biss" described how Sundays at Antioch were different to the other days of the week. Some of those Yankee soldiers from up North would sneak into civilian clothes and come to church at Antioch. Some of the Rebel soldiers did the same. They worshiped together, did not fight, and prayed to the same God. They sang beautiful songs together. One of the fellows from up North asked, "Why do you not have a church organ?" A Rebel in civilian clothes answered, "When the Indians chased the wagon train over the mountain, those Christians had to unload their wagons in order to outrun the Indians! They must have unloaded their organ." General conversation continued after the church service. An important question was, "If we're fighting over land, we can't take it with us to Heaven." Another suggested, "If we're fighting over the color of people, dark-skinned people make up most of the population. In fact, they make up a majority of people on earth. Why should they be our slaves?" "Uncle Biss" said, "Some of those soldiers must have agreed with Abraham Lincoln"...."Compromise, and keep the states together." In fact, after much bloodshed, that is exactly what happened. During the Civil War, Rebel soldiers walked along a Cherokee trail that led from Antioch north up over a long ridge and continued over the other side down to Gainesboro (settled in 1820). The Anderson, Johnson, Davis, Jones, McCoin, Davidson, Welch, Stewart, Brown, Bowman, Bennet, Pharris, Meadows, Maxwell, Spurlock, and Young families migrated to The Ridge after the Civil War.

A young medical doctor named McCoin established a medical clinic in his 21-room brick house on The Ridge after the Civil War. His daughter married a Davidson, who was also a doctor. The first little school in the community, naturally, was named after the McCoin family. The school became known as McCoinsville. The local church also took on the same name. The pillars of the community used the same building to conduct church services.

When James Carl's father died in 1936, the mules were sold to pay medical bills. Uncle Henry, a neighbor, gave the family a ride in an open-top Model-T Ford to the Big Meeting at McCoinsville. James Carl was five or six years old, but he can still remember how the preacher stomped the floor, screamed, and yelled; he "told it like it was." Later, a neighbor described it as "Hellfire and damnation preaching." It got results. Many sinners were converted to Christianity and were baptized in the cold muddy water of Flynn's Creek near Antioch. One almost drowned when the preacher's foot slipped. One night after a service, the Ford Model-T was not available. The family walked home from church. They passed another big meeting being held by another denomination and stopped and listened. The preacher pointed to the "fireworks high up in the sky" (the Northern Lights), and said, "The time has come!" About 30 people quickly repented. The preacher sped toward home to tell his wife of the great results, and ran off the road, across the ditch, and over a steep hill. His new Nash flipped over several times. As he described it the next day, he said to a drunk, "The Lord was with me or I would have been killed." The drunk asked, "Did it hurt the Lord?

The interest in big meetings grew. Apparently, McCoinsville led the way. Word got out that a black preacher from Nashville meant to hold a big tent meeting in Gainesboro in the fall of 1942. Many of the churches in Jackson County showed great interest. It happened and a logger made his flat-bed truck available. It was loaded six nights with families who wanted to "hear the word," and hear the word they did! When the preacher quoted Acts 2:38, one fellow, at church for his first time, thought he had said, "I have an axe and two thirty eights." His scare was bigger than the preacher who pointed to the Northern Lights. He warned with this type of scaring tactic, "The Japs have destroyed Pearl Harbor; they won at Battan, and they are sinking our war ships. They are coming after us. Get ready." He quoted scripture. He sang. He preached. He prayed. In brief, he showed many white preachers how to "spread the gospel." He even wore suits and ties. He spoke excellent English. He brought two 12-year old boys with him to be tutored. They did church songs without music, rock and roll style. In fact, after hearing these new-style songs, two local boys changed some words and came up with a new song for their Fourth of July musical contest on the square in Gainesboro, as follows:

"EVERBODY'S GONNA HAVE RELIGION IN GLORY"

Everbody's gonna have religion in glory.
Everbody's gonna to be singing a story.
Everbody's gonna have a wonderful time up there;
Glory hal-ah-lu-ya

You better get ready; you've been given a warning
It may be evening; it may be morning.
Everbody's gonna have a wonderful time up there
Glory hal-ah-lu-ya

All'll be free with streets of Gold
No deaths or sorrow, we've been told.
Everbody's gonna have a wonderful time up there;
A wonderful time up there.

The Jackson brothers from The Ridge gave much credit to Brother

Feeble, and his two preacher students, Bob and Frank, for bringing them a new idea for the next Fourth of July string music contest. Bob and Frank won first place!

Each of the two young preachers told the audience and vowed to Brother Feeble that they had decided to attend a college in Nashville and become ministers, evangelists, to be exact. Some of the white boys in the audience did not know that black boys could go to college. James Carl was twelve years old and thought, "If those black boys can go to college in Nashville, why can't I go to college in Cookeville?" However, he knew that he would have to hoe more corn or get better pay at the sawmill! He also had another idea….may be, he could find a better paying job. Luck came his way. When he became a senior in high school, he scored very high on an academic and physical dexterity test. A boot factory in Cookeville hired him at 80 cents an hour. The following year (1950) he had enough money to enter college. Sgt. Alvin C. York, in person, encouraged him to do so. He did.

James Carl enrolled at Tennessee Polytechnic Institute (TPI) in Cookeville, Tennessee. He lived at home, went to church on The Ridge, and drove to and from college. His transportation was a 1939, four-door Plymouth, and he recruited five passengers for the daily ride to and from Cookeville. Those passengers paid 50 cents each daily. That was $2.50 per day (25 hours of hoeing corn).

Sgt. York had said, "We are in a war in Korea to help those people become free." James Carl agreed with the thinking and enrolled in Military Science, Rural Officer Training Corps (ROTC). When he saw that black boys and girls were not allowed to enroll at TPI, he asked, "Why not?" Even though he attended a church on The Ridge, he was active in a church group on campus. He represented that group while debating on what was a hot topic in 1954….."Should or Should Not Black Students Attend White State Colleges?" He and his debate partner pleaded, "Yes." It was a bitter debate. One of the most popular ministers in Cookeville visited the church on The Ridge and tried to persuade him to drop out of that debate. He said, "No." The minister inferred that the Bible did not promote black students at TPI. James Carl reminded the preacher that the Bible infers that, "God is fair to all people." (God is not a respecter of persons.) Blacks are people. In addition, blacks pay taxes and should be eligible to attend TPI. The debate team from The Ridge and little Bloomington Springs, Tennessee, beat the heavy-weights from Detroit, Michigan, and Nashville, Tennessee. Again, the "Spirit of Americana" won. Later that year the U.S.

Supreme Court came to the same conclusion. Its historic decision, in the Brown vs. Board of Education, Topeka, Kansas, case, paved the way for black students to attend state universities.

In the midst of all the confusion about color, the McCoinsville school/church building on The Ridge burned. The congregation met in the shade of two huge pine trees throughout a hot summer. One Sunday, after the service ended, a little boy pointed out that twenty or thirty families rode to and from church in nice cars. Some of the cars even had automatic transmissions. "Why cannot those families throw dollar bills in the plate instead of quarters?" the little boy asked. Within weeks, plans were under way for citizens of The Ridge to build a new church building. James Carl was asked to type and mail letters asking for building donations. His first letter went to the community grocery store owner. His reply, "If it's going to be a wooden building, I'll give $100. If it's going to be brick, I'll give $1000 cash." When the pillars on The Ridge heard that, the decision was easy. His next letter went to David Lipscomb College in Nashville, Tennessee. The college sent $1000 and also encouraged its students to travel to The Ridge and preach. One of those fine young men became James Carl's brother-in-law. James Carl was asked to haul the bricks from Nashville, TN to build a modern church building. He did. He helped haul the red bricks with a 1936 Ford flat-bed truck and gave one month of labor (160 clock hours) toward the project. They must have overloaded that truck. A rear tire blew out. A TPI student stopped and used his jack to lift the truck and change the tire. He invited James Carl to ride to Fort Monmouth, New Jersey, the following week for Military Officer Basic Training. James Carl accepted.

When he returned to The Ridge for Christmas vacation, he learned that his debate partner had plans to marry another man (They were dear friends.). James Carl accepted an invitation to speak at TPI and describe Officer Training. Also, the Church on The Ridge asked him to lead the singing, say a prayer, and be the guest speaker. He did in full military dress uniform with Lieutenant Bars, Signal Corps Flags, and Expert Marksman badge. He was proud to be an officer helping with the service.

So, The Ridge helped to create a boot factory, build a new brick church building, promote Sgt. York's recruiting efforts, integrate TPI, and support the idea for citizens in South Korea to be free and democratic.

FROM LEFT: LOLA BETTY (LOFTIS) ANDERSON WHO WAS JAMES CARL ANDERSON'S MOTHER,
AVANA (LOFTIS) THOMPSON,
LEE LOFTIS AND NATHAN LOFTIS

The members of the Loftis family in this photo (1965) are daughters and sons of Pierce Loftis. Pierce was a direct descendent of Labin Loftis, a soldier under the command of General George Washington during the Revolutionary War. Following the War, Labin received land grant property on Roaring River near present day Gainesboro, Tennessee.

GRANDFATHER OF JAMES CARL ANDERSON
PIERCE WINCHESTER AND CLARA ROBERTS LOFTIS

Pierce Winchester was a direct descendant of
Labin Loftis who served with General George
Washington's Army during the Revolutionary War.

FOURTH AND ONE

Football first entered James Carl's life when he was a little boy at McCoinsville Elementary School on Route 3 (Highway 56) in Jackson County, Tennessee. His mother, on special occasions, would buy a "Knoxville Journal" or "Nashville Tennessean" newspaper, and he would read about the University of Tennessee and Vanderbilt football teams. However, some of the grown men and boys in those rural communities did not know about football in the 1930's and before.

Several years before there was a Tennessee Technological University or Dixie College in Cookeville, Tennessee, one of the first football games in the region was played between some boys from Cookeville and Sparta. The year was 1906. The game was played in a corn field between Gainesboro and Cookeville near the present day Hyder/Burks complex. The story goes that a rural farmer from near "No Man's Land" in Jackson County was riding a horse to Cookeville and witnessed a "brawl." He stopped his horse and watched the "fight" for ten minutes, and galloped his horse to the nearest sheriff's office. He told the lawman that ….

"About 22 men are in the biggest fight I have ever seen. If you don't get there in a hurry, somebody is going to be killed.

They are fighting over a ball. It's no longer round. They have mashed the ball until it's longer than it is across.

When one runs with the ball, he goes left and right as if he's drunk.

They knock each other to the ground. The fight is crazy. They fight furiously and then they're friendly, drink some water, and then they fight again.

One fighter kicked that mashed ball farther than I can throw a baseball.

53

Another boy carried the ball 80 yards and put it on the ground. Ten fellows jumped on top of him and screamed.

You must hurry. Take some deputies and go down there and
Stop the bloodshed!"

The rural back woodsman had witnessed, perhaps, the first football game ever played in the Upper Cumberland Region.

Soon after the football brawl in 1906, Dixie College was established in Cookeville, Tennessee, in 1915. Soon after that, Dixie College became Tennessee Polytechnic Institute (TPI). In the early years of college football in Cookeville, TPI attempted what many thought was an impossible task. The small college schedule included Vanderbilt University, which had a highly respected football program in 1939. Many of the TPI players were big, rough and tough boys from coal mining communities, farms, timber hills and hollows. Some had never been to Nashville. The story goes that TPI outplayed Vanderbilt until the last play of the game. It was time out and a long freight train was passing by near the football field. Apparently, some of the TPI players had never seen such a long train. Vanderbilt caught TPI off guard (perhaps watching the choo-choo train), and threw a long pass to tie little TPI 13-13!

Interest in football made its way from college down to high schools. Cookeville High School quickly developed, without doubt, the best high school program between Nashville and Knoxville. The Cookeville team was almost unbeatable until it played the Jackson County Blue Devils in the 1940's. The big Cookeville star running back was tall, heavy, quick, and as fast as lightning, Cookeville claimed. He was called "The Lone Train." By any measure, Cookeville High School was expected to win going away. At the end of the game, the score was Gainesboro 14 and Cookeville 6! The "Lone Train" was a bloody mess!

Many of the young men who played in this historic game were called up for World War II before the end of the school year. Some returned to finish high school after the war. By that time James Carl had become a high school senior at Jackson County Central High School. The team actually played against World War II veterans. In a game against Murfreesboro Central, ten of the players received medical treatment ... two with broken bones.

The high school had experienced winning seasons in the 1930's and 1940's. The principal and coaches scheduled their team to play, perhaps, the toughest schedule in the history of the school in the fall of 1948. Cookeville, Crossville, Livingston, Lebanon and Murfreesboro, without doubt, were some of the very best football teams in Tennessee. James Carl well remembers the game against Lebanon Central...a top rated football team. Their team featured an All-State tailback! Jackson County Central High School did not have an All-State player on its 1947 or 1948 team; however, it did have six Andersons. They were Ray, Walter, Billy, Jack, Paul, and James Carl. Some of these were descendents of families that traveled from Scotland to Boston, Massachusetts, i.e., Lawrence Anderson (1616 and one of first students at Harvard University, established in 1636) to Virginia to South Carolina to what is now Tennessee...Jackson County.... Cummings Falls Community to the Tom Anderson Farm and Blacksmith Shop ... Antioch Community ... to the James Bedford Anderson Farm and Mule Training Facility on "The Ridge" (Route 3) ... James Carl Anderson ... offensive and defensive right end on the 1948 Jackson County Blue Devils Football Team.

In the Lebanon game, the first play of the game, Lebanon Central sent four blockers shoulder-to-shoulder on a wide sweep play directly toward James Carl (right defensive end). They did him in, but the Jackson County team's line backer stopped the tailback after a short gain. During a time out, the line coach told James Carl what to do when those four players came at him again. Two plays later they did just that. Instead of meeting them nose to nose, James Carl laid his 6'2" body on top of their feet in a head-on fashion. They tumbled forward "to ass over elbow," and two outstanding linebackers threw the Lebanon Central All State tailback for a five yard loss! The game was on, and they were in it and how! Next, the football was turned over to the Blue Devils' team after a fourth and one play. The score was 0-0. The Blue Devils marched, on the ground, down the field. That bruising series could be described as blood and guts. The Blue Devils had one play that Lebanon Central High School could not stop on that first drive toward the goal line. It was twenty-one reverse. James Carl's job, on that play, was to block the opponents' big left defensive tackle. He had confidence because he was a senior and the defensive tackle was only a sophomore. When the ball was snapped, James Carl purposely let him commit forward and then blocked him sideways. It worked time and time again. When the Blue Devils were near the goal line, it was fourth down and one yard to the goal line. The Blue Devils' coach called for a time out and someone jokingly said, "Spit tobacco juice in their eyes." It is possible that one of the County Fair Tobacco Spitting Champions, a big offensive tackle, did just that! The offensive line was made up of farmers, loggers, hunters and spitting champions. They made a hole a Greyhound bus could have traveled through. The Blue Devils scored! A freshman kicked the extra point (his very first kick). Jackson County again beat one of the best teams in the state 7-6! After 60 years, that September, 1948, game is still talked about at class reunions and banquets. It's interesting to note that the 1948 football team was the smallest ever at Jackson County Central High School (averaged only 160 pounds per player). However, it was, perhaps, one of the fastest high school football teams in Tennessee during the 1948 season. Also, the team was loaded with Scottish talent! Seven team members went on to excel in university sports. Some set university and conference records in track and field events and football. The men of Kings Mountain, in South Carolina, planted some good genes that migrated across the Appalachian Mountains to what is now Tennessee.

There is a correlation between South Carolina's rag tag Army on Kings Mountain and the underdog 1948 Jackson County Blue Devils. Each time, a vicious ground attack achieved their goal to win. The element of surprise helped. The Scots of South Carolina at Kings Mountain utilized some of the best weapons available (very long-barreled flint-lock rifles). The Jackson County Blue Devils featured seven future university varsity athletes (weapons galore). Last, but not least, in both cases "Scottish blood was on the line." In each case, the heavily-favored team lost. In the case of Great Britain, General Ferguson was killed, and 800 South Carolina rag tag soldiers whipped 3000 Red Coats and ran them northward toward Canada. The underdog, Jackson County Blue Devils, beat the mighty Lebanon Central team who wore white jerseys and played with a white football! Jackson County in 1948 did not have a marching band. However, its football players played to the music of a 100-piece Lebanon High School Band and on fourth down and one yard to go scored and won 7-6!

AVERY TRACE, FIRST PUBLIC ROAD FROM EAST TENNESSEE TO THE FORT NASHBORO AREA

Avery Trace descended from The Ridge to Flynn's Creek and passed just north of present-day Nann Rash Cemetery to the fresh water branches that drained into the Creek. Legend has it that Native Americans attacked some of the wagon trains traveling along this route and leaving a high casualty rate. In fact, some of the casualties may have occurred on the same hillside as the Nann Rash Cemetery. Avery Trace was in the creek bed at times. The above scenes show descent from The Ridge to Flynn's creek and the westward route toward Fort Blount and the Cumberland River (late 18th Century)

COUNTRY MUSIC ON THE RIDGE

Many states and communities claim that "down home" country music originated in their area. However, James Carl disagrees and offers data to support the claim. Prior to 1941, there were only four radio stations in Tennessee that broadcast country music. The two successful radio stations in those days were WSM in Nashville and WHUB in Cookeville. WSM in Nashville promoted country music at its best via the Grand Ole Opry. However, James Carl points out that most of the singers and instrument players on the Grand Ole Opry were very good before they starred on the Opry. The situation left it wide open for rural areas to produce country music stars beside country roads, on hill sides, and in the woods. It happened, and how!

Perhaps one of the most rural areas in Tennessee during the early days of the twentieth century was The Ridge. This area was so depressed that some of the land was unclaimed. For example, No Man's Land was not claimed by anyone because no one wanted to pay property taxes on the land. The man who married James Carl's baby sitter introduced electricity in a house to the residents on The Ridge. This young man had worked on Ford Model-T and Model-A cars. He knew how to convert DC electricity to AC. He harnessed a water stream on his farm to a water wheel made from a bicycle wheel. He connected the wheel to a generator, converted the electricity to AC and sent electricity to his house with two strands of wire. People came from far and near to see electric lights in a rural house on The Ridge.

At age nine in 1940, James Carl took a car battery 1.8 miles in his little red Radio Flyer wagon to his friend's place where he charged the battery and James Carl's entire family listened to the Grand Ole Opry on Saturday nights. They charged batteries and listened to the Grand Ole Opry until the Tennessee Valley Authority and the Rural Electrical Association made electricity available for their rural house in the mid 1940's. Oakley Johnson bought an electric guitar and helped form the Johnson Country/Bluegrass/ Gospel Band.

The electric guitar player, his son, father, two sisters, a brother and a nephew formed the "Henry Johnson Band." This band on The Ridge rehearsed one evening each week and attracted large audiences. The band also did a country music program each week on WHUB in Cookeville, Tennessee. The instruments consisted of two guitars, a fiddle, banjo, mandolin, rub board, and homemade bass instrument.

The following songs were well received on The Ridge and over WHUB: "You Are My Sunshine," "Old Ninety Seven," "Wabash Cannon Ball," "She'll Be Coming Around the Mountain," "Good Old Summer Time," "Farther Along," "Life's Evening Sun," and "Flower in the Wild Woods."

The Johnson Band had opportunities to go "Big Time." They all had pretty good jobs and chose to live on The Ridge. However, they did do one wild tour of the Smoky Mountains and performed along the way. Members of the band took two Ford Model-A cars, welded the bodies together and made the first limousine on The Ridge. The band toured the Great Smoky Mountains in this nine-passenger car. It had no top, and was named, "Please Don't Rain."

"UNCLE" HENRY JOHNSON'S STRING BAND

"Uncle" Henry Johnson, sitting, is seen playing his favorite tune, "Good Old Summer Time," just prior to one of his Saturday morning radio country/bluegrass shows on WHUB in Cookeville, Tennessee (1943). Left to right, Nathan, Henry's oldest son, played the fiddle. Edgar, Nathan's son, "blew the jug." Rozelle, Henry's daughter, age 92 at this writing, sang and played a mandolin. Francis, Henry's daughter, sang and played a guitar. Oakley and Vestel, not shown, played electric and flat-top guitars, respectively. Charles, Oakley's son, not shown, often played a homemade #2 washtub bass-stringed instrument. James Carl Anderson, a neighbor boy and not shown, often appeared as a guest and help sang "Flower in the Wild Woods," and "You Are My Sunshine." James Carl's very first stage appearance of any kind was with the Johnson Band. They asked him to sing "You Are My Sunshine," and help the band perform "Flower in the Wild Woods." At age twelve in 1943-1944, he appeared two times as a guest and sang the songs requested.

Following his appearance with the Johnson Band, he helped two little neighbor boys rehearse to compete in the local Fourth of July Country and Gospel Music Contest in Gainesboro, Tennessee. They sang and played two gospel songs, participated in a tie-off, and won first place. Their three songs were "Camping in Canaan's Land," "Just A Little Talk with Jesus," and "Everbody's Gonna Have Religion in Glory."

Even though James Carl had sung with the Johnson Band at age 12, he did not own a musical instrument. While helping his mother clean a neighbor's house, they found a "throw-away" ukulele with a broken string. James Carl learned to make the notes of "When My Blue Moon Turns to Gold Again," with three strings. During the same summer, he worked at a nearby sawmill and made $2.00 per day. He saved his money and bought a used flat-top guitar for $13.00. It had six good strings. He learned some chords from an old, old paperback book. He thought he knew how to play that old guitar, but did not!

Nevertheless, one very wild country audience also thought that his younger brother, a neighbor boy, and James Carl knew how to play and sing. They did not know what they were doing, but the audience did not know that. They had had one too many!

The more they tried to sing and play, the more they thought they knew what they were doing. One sophisticated family in the neighborhood asked them to help celebrate a birthday, and that they did. James Carl's brother played his half-size accordion and James Carl played his $13.00 guitar. A house full of people sang. The birthday party got wild. The more they all sang, the louder it sounded. There must have been thirty visitors in that big living room. They took a corn cob out of a huge bottle and passed it from person to person. After a few loud songs, the bottle was empty! An old drunk spun the bottle. James Carl went round and round, and when it stopped, it pointed to the most popular girl at the party. He kissed her. The party was on!

The song "You Are My Sunshine" got the crowd's attention. At the end of "Flower in the Wild Woods," one could have heard a pin drop.

After the sad song, the party-prone audience requested "Old Ninety Seven." This old train song (a story about a bad train wreck in Tennessee) brought the crowd back to life. After a roar of laughter, they wanted "Wabash Cannon Ball." They got it and how!

The living room floor fell in. Mind you this was a big, new, well-built country house. The house stands to this day. James Carl and his brother had to work some extra days in a factory and on the family farm to repair that living room floor. That birthday party is still remembered by some of those who attended it in 1947. Perhaps, the party could be classified as a "Moonshine Classic."

After the wild birthday party experience, James Carl decided to become more civilized. He became a member of the local high school choir and enjoyed singing in church. His favorite choir songs were "Shine Little Glowworm Glimmer, Glimmer," "Kentucky Babe," and "Cruising Down the River." His first respected performance was at a classmate's funeral. He and three others sang "Amazing Grace" and "How Great Thou Art." After this sad experience, the school principal and choir director challenged James Carl. They asked him to plan a musical program to entertain the parents of the 1949 Senior Class at Jackson County Central High School in Tennessee.

James Carl had no telephone at home and asked to use the office telephone at school. It was his first long-distance telephone call in the Spring of 1949. The Jackson County Central High School had played Hendersonville High School in football two times and James Carl knew that June and Anita Carter attended that school. James Carl called their mother, Mother May Belle Carter. He asked her to bring her daughters to Gainesboro and entertain the parents of the school children. She hesitated until James Carl reminded her that the two high schools had something in common....football and music. She accepted with one exception. She asked James Carl to do a 30-minute "warm-up musical." He accepted. Chet Atkins drove her 1939 Buick limousine to Gainesboro. Charles Johnson and James Carl helped Chet set up the public address system. James Carl sang "Flower in the Wild Woods," "You Are My Sunshine" and "Cold, Cold Heart" while Joe and Sherrill Chapman accompanied him on the mandolin and flat-top guitar. Charles Johnson played the piano as James Carl sang "Cruising Down the River" and "Kentucky Babe." The first 30 minutes went well and Mother May Belle asked them to help do the concert. They helped her sing "Will the Circle Be Unbroken."

Following the concert, Mother May Belle asked Charles Johnson and James Carl to be guests on one of her programs in Nashville, but that did not materialize. James Carl had a driver's license, but no car. He was hired by the Atlas Boot Manufacturing Company in Cookeville, Tennessee, and his career took a whole new direction. After working as a stock clerk for almost two years, he was recommended by Sgt. Alvin C. York to become a Rural Officer Training Corps (R.O.T.C.) student at Tennessee Polytechnic Institute in Cookeville. He studied Military Science for four years at Tennessee Tech and became a commissioned officer in the U.S. Army Signal Corps in 1954.

Sgt. York was not the only person to have a significant influence on James Carl's career. Mr. Pete Williamson, his general science teacher and football coach, shouted one day in class, "The flag pole is on fire!" James Carl was the first student to the window. The teacher described it as slow oxidation. From that day forward James Carl's interest in science has never dwindled. The year was 1945. Two atomic bombs had just forced the Japanese to surrender. The teacher explained atomic fission!

After the football team beat one of the best teams in Tennessee, this teacher and coach told James Carl, "Pound for pound, you are one of the best I have ever coached." After James Carl's older brother had been found dead on a lonely, dark highway, that coach wrote in James Carl's school annual, "Do not pull in your wings because of a breeze, keep sailing." James Carl's last visit with this outstanding teacher was in a nursing home. His vision was very poor. He asked James Carl to help him "see" some of the unusual formations being used on football defense and offense. James Carl supplied his vision.

While attending Tennessee Tech, James Carl spent summers working for Chrysler Corporation, General Motors, and United Engineers, Inc., in Michigan. Even that was not enough money, and he sold his guitar to help pay tuition and campus expenses. Clay Anderson, James Carl's first cousin, bought the guitar for his son, Raymond. James Carl showed Raymond how to make three chords (G,C, & D) for gospel and country songs. He took it from there and later traveled and played with Bill Monroe's Blue Grass Band!

After James Carl completed his tour of active military duty, he was employed by Oak Ridge Associated Universities in Oak Ridge, Tennessee, as a Traveling Teacher Demonstrator for ten years. Next, he helped the State of Washington establish a State Energy Office. During that job, the personnel office of Combustion Engineering, Inc., in Windsor, Connecticut, called and invited James Carl for an interview. He flew there, was interviewed and hired. During the next six years, he helped some world-renowned scientists and engineers create TV video training tapes on nuclear steam supply systems and environmental protection systems for coal-burning electrical power plants. Combustion Engineering, Inc. was sold to a European country, and James Carl went back to school. He took graduate courses in education at the University of Tennessee and accepted a job as Supervisor of Education in Jackson County, Tennessee. After twenty very successful years as an adult educator for Jackson County, he retired. Then he took his very first formal guitar lesson.

After six lessons, he volunteered to sing and play the guitar in local nursing homes and assisted living facilities. A retirement home in Knoxville, Tennessee, gave the program an excellent rating. Morningside Assisted Living facility in Cookeville, Tennessee, has sponsored several of his 45-minute sessions of sing-along and solo selections.

Perhaps, the highlight of his very brief musical vocation has been at Morningside in Cookeville. The audience is composed of residents who cannot drive to Nashville to the Grand Ole Opry. Chris Roberts, James Carl's instructor, helped him revise his theme song, "Flower in the Wild Woods" on April 26, 2006, as follows:

"It was in the month of June, and the roses were in bloom,
when he took her in his arms so tenderly;
so by these words please remember me."

You're the flower that is blooming in the wild woods.
You're the flower that is blooming there for me.
Sweeter than the morning dew, and I will always love you.
You're the flower that is blooming there for me.

He set sail across the sea, where he met the enemy.
There was heartache when they sank his battleship.
A letter proved her deepest fears; she kept reading through her tears,
Those last words that were on her loved one's lips
(Repeat chorus)

McCOINSVILLE'S MILITARY HEROS

Long before there was a State of Tennessee, the English Crown had an agreement with the American native Indians not to send white settlers west of the Appalachian Mountains. However, a group of Scottish settlers went west to gain their freedom from excessive taxation and harassment from England, Spain, and other countries. Some of the Anderson families who traveled westwards had blood lines that could possibly be traced back to Anders and his son in Sweden. This freedom-hungry bunch settled in South Carolina's roughest hill country. They developed internal trade, taught work skills by apprenticeship, became excellent hunters, reared large families, farmed the land, fed grass to animals, and built grist mills and foundries. They designed long-barreled flint-lock rifles that were far superior to the British rifles. These rifles had a range of 500 to 800 yards! Also, they knew how to aim and fire those rifles. They were not afraid of "Red Coats."

The American Colonies lost those first few years of the Revolutionary War in the 1770's; that is, until England's General Ferguson threatened the Scottish settlement with death and torture if they did not surrender to his forces. Eight hundred Scottish farmers, blacksmiths, tradesmen, and a support group met in the middle of the night and planned an attack on Ferguson's Army. The Scottish "Clan" marched at night through woods, briars, underbrush, across creeks and marshes until they were within 500 yards of the British soldiers. They encircled the British and opened fire. After three hours of fierce battle more than 800 British soldiers lay dead. The Scots had only 26 casualties. Those long-barreled rifles got the job done and how! The Scots teamed up with General George Washington and his exhausted Army and chased the "Red Coats" all the way to Canada.

The settlers firing those long-barreled rifles could pick off the Indian scouts from a long distance. The Indian scouts were showing the Red Coats through the forest and without the scouts the British were completely out of their league. The Indian scouts cooperated with the British because they did not want the settlers moving into their territory. This was actually guerilla warfare against the British from tree top branches, from behind rocks and ridges, and any other way to silently deliver the blow. Not only did the Scottish Community of King's Mountain win its freedom, all thirteen colonies won their freedom as well.

Many of those Anderson, Johnson, Jackson, and Jones families moved westward from South Carolina to the most isolated hills and hollows they could find in today's Tennessee. A crater site near present day Antioch provided rich, creek bottom soil for grass, corn, hay, and garden vegetables. The Avery Trace road from present day Knoxville to Nashville follows the creek from the crater site to what is today Flynn's Lick. Antioch on Flynn's Creek became a thriving community in the 19th century. Henry Johnson used water wheel power from Flynn's Creek to grind corn meal for corn bread. Tom Anderson operated a blacksmith shop to make mule and horse shoes from Model-T axles. Tom's father, Paul, had previously used oxen to move logs to a water mill at Cummings Mill to make lumber for buildings in the new Cookeville community. One of the earliest travelers over the new Avery Trace East-West Road was young Andrew Jackson, who hailed from North Carolina. He became a successful prosecuting attorney and attended numerous social and legal functions at Fort Blount and Williamsburg near what is today called Flynn's Lick. Jackson County was named after this great personality, Andrew Jackson, the seventh President of the United States of America.

Henry Clay had a deep-seated dislike, some say hatred, for this man. When Andrew Jackson first started his political career, Henry Clay compared him to a donkey, expecting to ridicule him. However, the donkey was an animal highly respected for his hard work and strength by the rural population in Andrew Jackson's districts. Andrew Jackson took the symbol and made it his own and that is how the Democratic Party got the donkey as the party's symbol. Andrew Jackson lost his first attempt to become President, but won on his second try.

At least Andrew had a mule. Another man who walked to Tennessee (He didn't have a mule.) and could barely read or write, married the girl who tutored him. He also became President of the United States of America. He was Andrew Johnson.

Some of the first families of the Antioch Community were named Allen, Bennet, Anderson, Billingsley, Birdwell, Chaffin, Flat, Fox, Hale, Jones, Kirby, Loftis, Locke, Malone, Spurlock, and Williams; names still well known in this area.

As the population grew along Flynn's Creek, the younger population moved to higher ground – The Ridge. One of the first settlements three miles north of Antioch became known as McCoinsville. It got its name from Dr. McCoin who built a 21-room brick mansion there and brought the first Ford Model-T to the dirt road community. Early McCoinsville featured a wooden school building, grocery stores owned and operated by Bernice West, Fred Young, and Fred Anderson, and a Church of Christ congregation which met on Sunday afternoons in the school building. Henry moved his grist mill from Flynn's Creek water mill site to a new building out on The Ridge and powered the turning rocks with a Ford Model-T engine (later a Model-A engine). Corn and tobacco became the "King" money crops. Corn was marketed by the bushel and the "gallon." Tobacco was commercialized and sold by the carton.

The McCoinsville Community grew rapidly. When a big church meeting served dinner on the ground, visitors from Center Grove, Dudney's Hill, Antioch, Forks of the Creek, New Salem, Union Hill, Freewill, Flynn's Lick, and, sometimes, Gainesboro, attended. The school building was not big enough to hold such outings. They happened outside!

On the Saturday night before, the Johnson family treated those same families to country and bluegrass musicals. Frazier Moss was a guest performer and won some state and National fiddle contests. The Henry Johnson Family Country Music Band was second to none in Upper Cumberland and among the best in Tennessee. "Uncle Henry" played the banjo and sang, "Good Old Summer Time," "The Wreck of Old 97," and "Wabash Cannon Ball." Nathan, Henry's son, played the fiddle and led gospel songs. Francis, Henry's daughter, played a flat-top guitar and sang. Rozelle, Henry's daughter who is 90 years old and still alive at this writing, played a mandolin and sang. Edgar, a grandson, played a bass fiddle made of a #2 washtub, wood, and a strong steel string. Charles Johnson, a grandson, and James Carl were little boys who appeared as guests and helped the band sing, "You Are My Sunshine," "Flower in the Wildwoods," and "Cold, Cold Heart."

McCoinsville and The Ridge Community have never been the same since December 7, 1941. Japanese fighter bombers hit Pearl Harbor and the U.S. declared war. Germany sank several U. S. ships and tried to help

Japan win its war. The U.S. also declared war on Germany. Hundreds of young men in Jackson County were drafted and ordered to train and prepare to fight the enemy. Many of the young men from Jackson County lived in or near the McCoinsville Community. For example, Herman C. Anderson, James Carl's oldest brother, and Tom C. Bennet worked together at a molasses mill. They were both quickly drafted. Ernest Spurlock, James Carl's brother-in-law, who lived on a nearby farm, was drafted a few months later. Herman passed the physical and became a medical technician with the rank of Staff Sergeant. He served in Africa, Sicily, Italy, France, and became a prisoner of war in Germany. He survived the war, but never returned to good health. Tom C. failed the physical two times, but passed when soldiers were badly needed. He could shoot a rabbit hopping at full speed. He also built a small "trailer truck" from a Ford Model-A car and pieces of a farm wagon. One of his last firewood deliveries, prior to being drafted, was to James Carl's mother, a widow with six children at home. Tom C. died in a burning Army tank in France near the end of World War II. Ernest Spurlock received special training at Camp Cook, California, and repaired damaged U.S. Army tanks in France for General Patton's army. Many soldiers from the McCoinsville Community attended Johnson Band musicals on Saturday nights during World War II. The band rehearsed its weekly WHUB radio program. Large crowds attended each rehearsal. The Mahaney families of New Salem attended regularly. Garret Mahaney was the first serviceman from Jackson County to be killed in the war. He boarded with Ernest and Virdia Spurlock in Merced, California, prior to entering the U.S. Navy. He was, indeed, a young hero. Henry Mark Jones, a neighbor and also a sailor, was killed in battle against the Japanese. Donald Loftis, James Carl's cousin, graduated from high school and joined the U.S. Army. He talked with James Carl, at length, during his furlough at a Johnson Band Musical. He was shipped off to France and was killed by German machine fire within a few weeks.

HEADSTONE FOR STAFF SERGEANT HERMAN C. ANDERSON
January 24, 1917 – February 27, 1949

Staff Sergeant. Herman C. Anderson - U.S. Army Medical Corps (1917-1949). Served in WWII - USA, England, North Africa, Sicily, Italy, France and Germany - German prisoner 9 months - Purple Heart, Bronze Star, several battle stars.

James Carl was only twelve years old at the time and these neighborhood boys were his "big brothers." The late Carson Maxwell was his closest friend in high school and college. Charles Maxwell, his brother, was killed in the war. A neighbor, during his furlough after completing basic training in the U.S. Army, insisted that he would rather die on U.S. soil than in Europe or the Pacific. Apparently he ran his 1934 Ford into a big tree at top speed. The V-8 engine was jammed back under the front seat. James Carl helped get him out of that car. He died on U.S. soil – not a war hero, but a victim of war just the same. While the McCoinsville neighbors were being killed in the war on a steady basis, James Carl talked to Ben Price, who survived the sinking of the U.S. Hornet and U.S. Wasp in the South Pacific. He said, "You're young and I hope you don't have to be in a war as I've been. Those Japanese are good fighters." He was discouraged, but lived to become a winner. The U.S. Hornet, his ship, paid the supreme price, but sent B-25 Mitchell Bombers to Tokyo and upset Japan's apple cart. Perhaps that mission marked the turning point in World War II in the South Pacific. Numerous other servicemen of the McCoinsville Community survived World War II. Some lost limbs, eyes, kidneys, and other body parts. The community was convinced that freedom was not cheap.

Soldiers had hardly put their uniforms away before their younger brothers and sisters prepared to fight in Korea. Apparently the citizens of South Korea chose freedom over communism and fought to defend their choice. The U.S. chose to help South Korea practice democracy and freedom. It was called a military conflict; however, James Carl disagreed. He believes it was and is a war and had some fellow soldiers suffer and die near the 38th Parallel. In fact, U.S. service men defend the 38th Parallel to this day.

James Carl graduated from Jackson County Central High School in 1949 and accepted a stock clerk position with Atlas Boot Manufacturing Company in Cookeville, Tennessee, at 17 years old. Mr. Harry Vice, the company president, and Bill Holloway, his purchasing agent, were excellent co-workers. In the Spring of 1950, while helping a Mason & Dixon truck driver unload leather, a tall, 280-pound man tapped James Carl on the shoulder from behind. Rather than swinging, he decided to behave. The man was none other than Sergeant Alvin C. York. He was in Cookeville to accept a special pair of cowboy boots and to help Tennessee Polytechnic Institute (TPI), a four-year college, establish a Rural Officer Training Corps (R.O.T.C.). He highly encouraged James Carl to go across town that very day and enroll. James Carl had read the book, "Alvin C. York," and had played football against one of his sons. He took that advice and enrolled at TPI.

The same summer that war was raging in Korea, a new baseball league was formed in the Upper Cumberland Region. The McCoinsville Community sponsored "The Ridge Runners Team." The team was composed of Carl Anderson, Clarence Anderson, James Paul Anderson, Carson Maxwell, Harold Martin, Douglas Johnson, Charles Johnson, Roy Petty, David Petty, Ralph Pippin, Earl Brown, and Carl Brown. The league consisted of six teams. Norman Clark managed the "Glad Dice" team. His was the best team in the league. For example, Fid Dixon was recruited by the Detroit Tigers. The entire league came to a halt when most of the athletes were classified "1A" in the military draft.

James Carl left the Ridge Runners team and studied Signal Corps R.O.T.C. at Tennessee Tech where he earned a Bachelor of Science Degree and served as a Signal Corps Officer. Douglas Johnson was drafted, stayed in the military as his career, and retired as a Sergeant 26 years later. Harold Martin was drafted as a Private, came out, attended college, re-enlisted and went to Officers' Candidate School and retired 26 years later as a Lt. Colonel. Clarence Anderson served 43 years in the U.S. Army National Guard and retired as a Captain. Carson Maxwell studied R.O.T.C. at Tennessee Tech, majored in Agriculture and played the big drum in the Tennessee Tech Marching Band. James Carl helped him transport the big drum to and from some of the OVC football games. He served as a First Lieutenant during the Korean War era. Carl Brown and Roy Petty served with honor in the U.S. Army. Combat injuries may have contributed to Carl Brown's early death.

When war broke out in Korea in 1950, R.O.T.C. Instructors suggested that it was a "Police Action" and part of a long cold war. War it was... North Koreans started fighting South Koreans. China's soldiers helped the North Koreans. The U.S. and its allies helped South Korea. Fred Maxwell, a resident of The Ridge, knew it was a war. He had lost a brother in World War II and he knew lives were being lost in Korea.

The library in Gainesboro was named in honor of Charles Holland who was killed in military action in Korea. The library is only three miles from The Ridge. Ben Stone of Jackson County was also killed in Korea. A Cumberland River Bridge, four miles from The Ridge, was named in honor of him. Based on what happened to young men and women in uniform in Korea, the 1950-1953 so-called "Police Action" or "Conflict" was, indeed, a war.

History may have neglected the importance of military service of the men and women who served between the Korean War and the Vietnam War. Service men and women of that era played key roles in keeping this country free. For example, Captain John B. Jones of McCoinsville, a Navigator in the U.S. Air Force, supervised missions in B-36 Bombers near the Soviet Union borders between communist and democratic countries of Europe. His plane and its cargo were capable of crippling any country on the face of the earth. His responsibility was immense. He and his language team intercepted Soviet conversations and advised the U.S. military of Russia's military plans.

At the time, James Carl was a First Lieutenant with the Fifth Army, 529th Signal Company. Capt. Jones met him more than once and discussed how communications could be improved within the military worldwide. At the time (1955-1956), there were no communications satellites. They had to rely on wire and radio communications. They practiced long distance teletype and voice communications with ANGRC 26 (Army, Navy, Ground, Radio Communications) and relay equipment from the covered bed of a two and one half ton Dodge truck that had double dual wheels on the rear. Also, Colonel Niland, Major Peterson, and General Watlington designated James Carl to coordinate with the RCA Corporation and build a Rhombic Antenna high on a mountain in Colorado to net eastward with the U.S. Air Force and U.S. Naval Fleet and westward to the Pacific fleet. This wide range plan proved to be very effective. The entire plan was classified at that time as TOP SECRET.

The concept was tested during Sagebrush War Games in Louisiana in 1955. The training was costly. Thirteen young men lost their lives during that tough training in muddy forests infested with alligators and coral snakes. An acquaintance from the Officer's Club, in Fort Carson, Colorado, was bitten by a coral snake during Sagebrush training and died within hours. This Sagebrush training, without a doubt, helped pave the way for ANGRC communications during the Vietnam War which may have been won or may have been lost. After Sputnik (1957), satellites paved the way to relay radio, teletype, and computer communications much more effectively. However, the communications efforts had to '"crawl before they could walk" in terms of communicating. Young service men and women from McCoinsville helped the United States of America to crawl. Some of these men became career military men and helped the U.S. develop the best military force in the world.

JAMES BEDFORD ANDERSON, (1890-1936)
AND LOLA BETTY (LOFTIS) ANDERSON (1895-1966)

WITH HERMAN C. ANDERSON (1917-1949)
ON HIS FIRST BIRTHDAY

Both little girls and boys on The Ridge wore
dresses until about 4 years of age.

...True Americans Proudly Succeed
TAPS
"Day is done, gone the sun,
From the lakes, from the hills,
From the sky, all is well,
Safely rest, God is nigh."

Words from TruthOrFiction.com

JAMES CARL'S FAMILY
VISITED THE RIDGE

James Carl completed his tour of active duty in the U.S. Army, completed his Masters Degree at the University of Colorado, and presented high school assemblies' programs for a few years with Oak Ridge Associated Universities. In 1963, James Carl did a TV series of 30-minute programs live on WATE TV in Knoxville, Tennessee, called "Children and Science." A fifth-grade class in Oak Ridge, Tennessee, watched "Atoms and Elements" and "Molecules and Compounds." Their teacher, Mary Ann Roselli, of Everett, Massachusetts, called him and asked him to visit her fifth grade class and answer some questions. These sessions went very well. Mary Ann and James Carl spent time in libraries, playing volleyball, attending college concerts, and, yes, to The Ridge.

Mary Ann was a beautiful and intelligent woman. Her parents were from England and Italy. The old grist miller across the road from where James Carl grew up said, "She shore is purty, and she don't chew, but is she our kind?" James Carl told him most definitely, "Yes." Mary Ann let him know in no uncertain terms that "she was after him" and not those guys from Moonshine Island. This was her first visit to The Ridge. Mary Ann and James Carl were married July 3, 1965.

When James Carl's mother died of a stroke in early 1966, Mary Ann and James Carl sat beside the graves of his parents and grandparents. Their first child, Kim, was born in Tennessee on May 24, 1966. They moved to Olympia, Washington, three months later. Their son, Michael, was born in Olympia in August of 1967. James Carl had a good civil service job until Combustion Engineering, Inc., called him from Windsor, Connecticut.

He flew there, was interviewed, and accepted a job as Coordinator for Sales Training. He helped Dr. Walter Zinn and Harold Litginberger, two world-famous scientists, develop TV training tapes for fifty-five sales engineers. Mr. Joe Singer also helped with the work.

Vacations were wonderful family outings at Niagara Falls, Plymouth Rock, and Boston, Massachusetts, during those first few years. Then they planned a vacation to The Ridge. In a new Ford Pinto station wagon they drove south on the new Interstate 81 and I-40. The mountains, valleys, and vegetation were beautiful. Kim and Mike quickly learned to like Southern-cooked food. They spent night #2 in Nashville, Tennessee. They enjoyed the Grand Old Opry so much they sat through two complete shows. Dolly Parton and Porter Waggoner stole the show. James Carl picked up "Green, Green Grass of Home." The next day they visited the Tennessee State Capitol, the Parthenon, and their Uncle Clarence Anderson, who worked for the state of Tennessee.

Next on the schedule was a visit to The Ridge in Jackson County (named for President Andrew Jackson.). They had planned a full three-day visit and spent the first one hunting stone-age tools, Indian arrow heads, and walking over the 97-acre farm. The second day they visited farm animals, the old miller across the road and a host of cousins and neighbors. They sang ballads and country songs. The third day they borrowed Prince, a big, friendly dog, and set out over some very steep, rough hillsides. Kim's foot slipped and she started to fall over a high vertical drop. Prince caught her pant leg and held on for dear life until James Carl rescued Kim and Prince. From that day forward, Kim liked animals, especially dogs and cats. Six-year old Mike was very athletic and enjoyed the rough paths and trails through the woods. Finally, they reached their destination....the waterfall. After a two-day rain, the waterfall was exciting and only one hundred yards upstream from Moonshine Island. The children learned about their dad at age 10 hoeing corn downstream for 60 cents a day. They also heard about catching animals and selling the furs, which they thought was cruel. All three enjoyed the wonderfully scenic trip back to Connecticut.

After his employment with Combustion Engineering, Inc., James Carl did presentations on nuclear energy for ten years. He and his two children enjoyed excellent visits with one another. Kim visited European countries on two occasions while on tour with her Uncle Craig. Mike visited James Carl several times down South and out West. Mike decided to write about the most enjoyable aspects of his traveling. These are his exact words:

Funny Stories from my travels with Dad:

1. Because I grew up in Connecticut and my Dad moved back to Tennessee when I was 9 years old, I did not see him as often over the years as we would have liked. That being said, when you don't see someone as much it tends to make the times you spend together memorable, and it may have helped keep some of the times we've shared together more vivid in my mind than they would have been otherwise. This chapter describes some of the more memorable times we shared over the years, with a focus on some of the adventures we've had together.

2. My Dad greatly enjoyed playing matchmaker with me when I was a teenager. Various "dates" I had while at my Dad's hotel he stayed in when visiting where I lived:

- When I was 15 my Dad actually set me up with a 27-year-old flight attendant. We went for a jog around the hotel parking lot one afternoon and supposedly were going to get together the next evening. She stood me up and Dad said she showed up in the hotel lounge that evening with a pilot.

- One night at the same hotel, as my Dad headed out the door of our room to go to the lounge I told him "send me back a date" not thinking this was a real possibility. A while later I was in the room watching a football game when there was a knock on the door. I assumed it was my Dad and opened the door wearing only shorts and did not even bother to look at who it was. I walked back to watch TV and in comes a nice looking girl about my age and says "your Dad sent me." We talked for a few minutes and I helped her sneak back to her room as she had broken curfew and her tour organizers were searching for her.

- For my 16th birthday party my Dad convinced a bunch of girls swimming at the hotel pool that they should toss me into the pool in honor of my birthday. They did and my Dad told them to throw my friend in as well. Before they could do it, however, my friend jumped in the pool all by himself.

3. My Dad has a unique way of throwing a rock which is hard to describe, but it involves wedging a small rock within the

joints of a bent pointer finger and using finger, wrist, elbow and shoulder levers to accelerate the rock. It leaves his fingers with so much force it makes a whizzing noise, and, as I will describe, can be quite accurate. While at Rock City Gardens in Chattanooga my Dad picked up a rock and took aim at a goat sleeping on a rock about 20 yards away. Not believing he would hit it, I did not worry too much. His first shot hit the goat square on the head making a loud noise and startling the daylights out of the goat.

4. When I had just turned 17 my Dad and I flew to Paris on a week's vacation. Hotel and airfare were free for both of us based on reward points my Dad had earned from staying in a hotel chain's properties more than 75 nights the previous year. The trip was an unbelievable experience on many levels and one that I clearly remember despite it being more than 25 years ago.

5. Neither my Dad nor I spoke French, but we got to talking with a student from the University of Sorbonne on the plane from New York to Paris and it was funny listening to my Dad learn a few words and pronouncing them with a Southern accent. But, of course, traveling to a city such as Paris, speaking English is typically enough to communicate as needed. When we first arrived at Orly Airport, we got in a taxi to take us to our hotel. We both were excited, thinking our hotel was going to be near there as we got closer and closer to downtown and passed within a short distance of the Eiffel Tower. But we kept on driving and ended up at our hotel right next to the other major Paris airport, Charles De Gaulle. Not as good as downtown, but it was free! The neighborhood next to our hotel was very interesting to both of us. We spoke to an older woman who showed us the remains of stone walls that had been destroyed during World War I fighting, when she was a young girl 70 years earlier.

6. Another interesting historic discussion we had was at a World War II Memorial in Paris. We were there on the 40th anniversary of the liberation of Paris, so there was much discussion regarding World War II, with a focus on everything from D-Day to Paris liberation and beyond. At this memorial my Dad started a discussion with an English veteran that was

several years older than my Dad and had fought in World War II. Turned out the English veteran and my Dad's brother, Herman, had both landed in France on D-Day, and for all we knew may have crossed paths while liberating France. They looked at an invasion map and compared where each had been, reflecting on contributions made in such a momentous struggle.

7. While in Paris, my Dad made another miracle rock throw. One afternoon while walking across the city, we happened to be on a wide avenue that had an empty lot across the street. It also had a traffic sign next to the empty lot. My Dad came across a perfect size rock and said, "Watch this." He then fired the rock at the traffic sign, hitting it squarely, making a loud ringing noise, and startling others that did not see what happened, but figured the loud noise could pose some danger. He made sure when he threw it that no one would get hit, but that did not guarantee it would not scare anyone!

8. One day while in Paris we took a stroll through one of the famous department stores and came across a money exchange counter. When we got to the front of the line my Dad handed the clerk $80 and the clerk handed him approximately 65 francs in return. I had studied the exchange rate before the trip (more than 8 francs per dollar at the time) and told my Dad that he should get 650 francs, not 65. Clearly they were for some reason moving the decimal place one digit over. He then complained to the clerk who repeatedly claimed she had done the math correctly. My Dad insisted she speak to a manager, but the manager agreed with the clerk. My Dad was not going to get cheated, and he gave them back the 65 francs, reached under the grill and grabbed his $80 back, and we went right across the street and got 650 francs from a bank instead! Maybe it was a one-time mistake, but we could not help but think how many tourists were unaware they were not receiving the right amount.

9. When I was 12 years old I told my Dad that my Mom let me drive with her in the car so he let me get behind the wheel of his Maxi-van. I was scared to death, had little idea what I was doing, and crawled all the way from Windsor to Simsbury, Connecticut, with a long line of traffic tailgating me all the

way home. I'd say we were both lucky I made it home without running off the road. Two years later I drove the van all the way across Kansas on one of our cross country adventures. By then I had an idea what I was doing.

10. My Dad had an instructor's pilot's license and he and I would go flying on occasion. This one may be hard to believe, but I can remember when I was 7 years old my Dad would actually let me hold the controls of a Cessna 172 Skyhawk while he snapped photos from the plane a few thousand feet above the ground. The plane had dual controls, with my Dad having the master controls, so he could have easily compensated if I made a mistake, but it was an interesting experience nonetheless.

11. Education has always been important to both of us and we have shared a number of experiences related to education. For example, my Dad worked for years lecturing utility companies and schools about the benefits of various types of power including both nuclear and natural gas. I enjoyed watching these lectures not only to see how much my Dad knew about these topics, but also because at times he would get sidetracked a bit by the audience, often because he had a southern accent that would get the attention of folks when traveling in other parts of the country. I remember one lecture to a relatively small group in Connecticut when one member of the audience asked my Dad where he was from. When he said Tennessee the audience member commented that there was some excellent college football in that part of the country. As soon as he said that, my Dad's eyes lit up as he described the passion of college football in Tennessee and said something like, "when all those folks come down out of the hills with their Jack Daniels and wearing their Tennessee Orange, there is always excitement." Any time one of his lectures got a bit more personal such as this, I thought it made for a better overall educational experience for all of them because it got more people's attention than a traditional technical lecture would.

12. While the Supervisor of Adult Education in his home county, I enjoyed helping him teach students and tutored some of his students in both academic and athletic pursuits over a number of years. I enjoyed helping out and seeing the respect he was given

for all of his efforts, and could clearly see the positive impact he was having on so many people's lives. Probably the greatest enjoyment related to the position that he had with the county for nearly 20 years was attending the graduation ceremonies when my Dad would be the Master of Ceremonies. It was obvious to me that the students, teachers, and supervisor were all justifiably proud of their accomplishments and positives were being realized from this educational program. I recall there was at least one year in which almost as many adults received G.E.D. certificates in my Dad's program as there were students that graduated from the county high school, which shows how many people were being helped.

13. The summer before my freshman year in college my Dad and I woke up one morning in Easton, Pennsylvania, and shot some 3 pointers with the basketball coaches at Lafayette where I had been recruited to play. We drove from there straight to a university in Virginia to catch up with my buddy who had been recruited to play there. He was in a summer basketball camp with other college players and they were one short for the next game. My friend asked if I wanted to play and I did. I played well and made the winning shot at the end of the game which prompted their coach to come up to me and ask me where I played ball. I told him where I was headed and he asked if I would be interested in going to a local prep school for a year with a possible basketball scholarship down the line. I declined, but found it interesting that the school was penalized by the NCAA for numerous NCAA recruiting violations not long after that day.

14. This was one of several drives that we made from the Northeast to Connecticut over the years, sometimes in one of my Dad's classic cars like a Galaxie, or one of his Lincolns, a brand of car he enjoys tremendously. One summer while I was in college he ended up having both a Lincoln and a Galaxie in the Northeast, and we ended up driving tandem back to Tennessee. Another time we stopped in The Meadowlands, New Jersey, to see the University of Tennessee win a very exciting football game against Iowa. That was the day I got hooked on Tennessee football and I've made a point of going to at least one game per year ever since the late 1980s. Regardless

of the specifics, it seemed these trips always had a few surprises and a few more laughs.

15. On one trip to Tennessee we were in a 1964 Ford Galaxie and as we left the highway in New Jersey steam started flying out of the hood of the car. There was so much steam coming out that it frightened some people in the Howard Johnson's restaurant whose parking lot we pulled into. Turned out it was only a failed radiator hose, but you'd never know it by the look in the eyes of the restaurant patrons.

16. In the summer of 1982 my Dad had arranged for us to paint his friend's house near Denver, Colorado. So we went over there, but when we arrived we realized painting the back of the house might be a problem because the friend had German Shepherds that did not like us being around. My Dad, however, always traveled with a cooler full of food. He grabbed a few slices of bologna and within minutes the dogs were our friends and we had no more problems painting the house.

17. Later on that same trip we drove up the winding road that leads to the top of Pike's Peak, Colorado. We did not see much from the top that day because the cloud cover was below the summit, but I remember while we were driving down the mountain a checkpoint had been set up to test people's brakes. An officer touched our brakes, burned his finger, cursed, and told us we better stop for a while and let the brakes cool down! Later, we noticed, as we drove the rest of the way down, that there were a number of turnoffs from the road that headed upward for people to use to help them stop if they should lose their brakes. Seems we might have used one, also, if not for the checkpoint.

18. On July 4, 1983, we were again at Pike's Peak and had decided to go up to the top of the mountain on the cog railway. At the bottom of the mountain it was a beautiful 80-degree day, but you could see that there was still a good amount of snow on the top of the mountain. While we waited for the train, a wife standing near us looked up at the snow and asked her husband whether or not it would be cold on top of the mountain and if they should get some warmer clothes out of the car because they were both wearing shorts and short sleeved shirts. Without even hesitating the husband said, "No,

it's closer to the sun up there." Well, they should have done a little research because when we got up toward the timber line everyone started closing the train's windows and it was clear it was going to be cold by the time we reached the top. When we got to the top, as I enjoyed a friendly snowball fight with some of the others on the train, the young couple made a mad dash toward the visitor's center with the temperature about 40 degrees and the wind chill much colder!

19. My Dad used to have fun doing yard sales and was quite the salesman. During one of these sales, a stray dog wandered up as a family that had purchased several items was getting ready to leave. My Dad convinced them to buy this dog, too, which he had never seen before, and we loaded the dog up with the other items and they were on their way!

20. Because my Dad got enjoyment out of yard sales and automobiles, the combination sometimes led to interesting situations. As the result of some "horse trading" my Dad at one time had a dune buggy that he liked to drive around the rural country roads where he lived. One day we were going for a ride and he told me there was a mean German Shepherd that lived nearby and had tried to attack him as he drove past in the dune buggy a few days earlier. He said that was why he kept a slingshot and rocks inside the vehicle. Sure enough, when we started down the highway the dog came seemingly from nowhere, barking like crazy, and rapidly approaching my side of the dune buggy. Good thing the dune buggy was well armed because it was clear the dog did not enjoy being on the wrong end of a good slingshot! That dog did not attack my Dad again, so I guess the lesson was effective!

HOLY CHICKENS AND
SHOTGUN HALLOWEENS

James Carl saw his Uncle Bob and Aunt Rose and their children, who were his first cousins, move to what was called the Homesteads in Crossville, Tennessee. The Homesteads was a government program assisting families farm and maintain a number of acres for a certain number of years and the property would then belong to the homesteader. James Carl's cousin, Polly, writes of a few family happenings during those times:

My mother looked out her kitchen window while she was peeling potatoes for dinner and saw her chickens wobbling around the back yard as though they were drunk, some flopping over and not getting up off the ground. She ran outside to see what could be wrong! Chickens meant eggs for breakfast and baking and meat for Sunday dinner. When her hens were setting on their eggs, she watched over them very carefully. When the chicks were hatched I can remember some kind of little box container that she kept warm with a light bulb so they would survive. Sometimes she slept in an upper room with a wood burning stove with the baby chicks in their boxes. When she woke up cold, she knew it was time to put more wood in the stove. She sold chickens and eggs for income. Chickens on our farm were very important to our livelihood.

At the corner of the farmhouse by the back porch was a rain barrel placed to catch rain running off the roof. This usually stayed pretty full of water and that water was important, too, because it could be used for watering the garden vegetables and other uses, saving the water from the cistern. We had a cistern for house water because no well had been dug. When she ran out the back screen door and looked around the corner of the house, she heard a child's voice very solemnly say, "I now baptize you in the name of the Father, the Son, and the Holy Ghost." Splash!! Another chicken got dunked in the water in the rain barrel. It seems my sisters (I had six, all older than I) had watched a recent baptism in a creek near our small country church and decided to make my mother's chickens Holy. They just about left this earth that day, but, fortunately, Mama saved the recently baptized and rescued those waiting to get their sanctification.

We attended a small country church where my father led the singing. Our church did not believe in having any music so Daddy would hold a harmonica to his mouth, blow the note for all to hear, and lead all the songs. When we traveled in the car, all nine of us, five sat in the back seat and four in the front seat, Daddy would start singing the hymns from church and my sisters would harmonize. One sister sang alto, two sang soprano, and Daddy chimed in on the bass notes once he got us started. I loved to sing, but could not find the right note to harmonize. The other four members of our family listened and enjoyed.

We lived on that particular farm for a number of years and would have stayed there for a life time, except for the tragedy of a fire. Daddy was homesteading 200 acres of prime farm land in Crossville, Tennessee. There was a forest on 2 sides of the farm house, a house with huge bedrooms, living room with fireplace, separate dining room, ample kitchen, and indoor bathroom (but no running hot water); the exterior was covered with crab orchard stone as were all the homes on the Homestead properties. Daddy had a barn for animals, a very large garden plot, and fields for corn, etc. The chicken house was close to the farm house. There were fruit trees in abundance. Everything a skilled farmer needed to maintain his home and family by putting his own sweat into his life.

When I was still of preschool age, I remember standing in an upstairs bedroom looking out the window and seeing a column of black smoke coming out of the woods. My mother had told me to go there and stay and not come out. THE WOODS WERE ON FIRE! Neighbors came to help. The cistern was pumped dry, using all the water to put out the fire so the house was not damaged. Equipment was brought in and wells were dug every place possible, but no water could be found to support the farm. Without that water, my dad lost his homestead forcing him to move to another location, still on the Homestead properties, but now my parents rented their home and Daddy lost the opportunity to own property there. We now had to walk to school because anyone who lived within a mile of the school house could not ride the bus. I remember one day walking home in a pouring rain and being passed by a church member in his 4-door car with ample room for all 7 of us to ride. Daddy solved that problem by moving us again, far enough away from the school so we could ride the bus. In this new house, we had a long, long driveway out to the road. The driveway was protected by a gate at the end. I have heard my sisters tell of being visited by their boyfriends while Daddy was at work (he worked 24 hour shifts, 24 hours on and 24 hours off). After the boys left the girls would use tree branches to sweep the driveway of tire tracks so Daddy would not know of the visits. No boys allowed!!

There was not a lot of social activity for young people except for church and some of the local boys liked to play pranks. On Halloween, Daddy went to town to help a relative with electioneering and all seven of us girls were home with Mama. We heard noises at the road. It seemed that some of those neighborhood pranksters were trying to take down our gate and throw it in a ditch as a Halloween joke. My mother would have none of that! She pulled Daddy's shotgun from its perch and shot twice in the air. After that, my older sisters were known at school as the "Shotgun Andersons."

ROBERT (BOB) ANDERSON AND WIFE, ROSE LEE (PHARRIS) ANDERSON

AND DAUGHTERS AT THEIR HOME ON "THE HOMESTEADS"

This family photo was made about 1944 near Crossville, Tennessee, on "The Homesteads," where the Anderson family lived from 1936 until moving to Oak Ridge, Tennessee, in 1946. The girls are from left to right, Dolan, Allene, Marie, Reba, Erlene, and Jewel. Polly is standing between her father and mother, seated. Dolan's twin sister, Doyal, passed away as an infant. Erlene and Allene are twins.

All the houses on the Homesteads were made with Crab Orchard stone as seen in this picture. The car belonged to the Anderson family and was used for the commute to work in Oak Ridge, Tennessee, until the family moved its home there.

But that night was not over. We had all gone to bed and were asleep. Mama called all the girls to her because she had heard a noise on the porch. The porch fit into the L-shaped corner of the house with a window from the master bedroom looking out on the porch. The front door was situated on the long side of the "L" with another window. Mama got that shotgun out again. She positioned herself on her knees by the side of the bed, propping herself up on her elbows with the gun pointed at the window. She told the older girls to go into the living room and flip on the porch light and when the light came on she would shoot whoever it was that was trying to get into the house. As soon as they flipped the switch, screams came from the girls shouting, "Mama, Mama, don't shoot! Don't shoot! It's Daddy! It's Daddy!" Daddy had come home very late and tried to get my mother's attention by scratching and knocking on the bedroom window, never expecting that he might be mistaken for an intruder, not knowing the earlier events of the day. Mama did not shoot and he came inside safely.

My mother was a woman of much courage and strength as were many women of her day, never praised or heralded. She always deferred to my dad, but in my memories I am amazed how she was able to do all the things required of her. She, for a time, washed clothes on a rub board and finally got a washing machine. She had six pregnancies, two of which were twin babies, eight babies in eight and one half years. One of those babies died as an infant before I was born. Seven girls grew to adulthood of which I am the youngest. She made all our dresses from flour sacks, which in those days came with a floral pattern. I don't remember ever having a store-bought dress when I was a child. I do remember one special dress made from a sateen cotton with a different design in which the bodice came down into the skirt in a v-shape and gathers all around and a huge sash in the back. She cut down coats from hand-me-downs for my older sisters. She never had straight pins, but used case knives to hold patterns in place while she cut material on the floor. I can remember her bent over the sewing machine putting those garments together. She did these things at night because all her days were too full to squeeze them in. She canned fruits and vegetables, rung heads off chickens and boiled them to be able to pick the feathers off, cooked a family meal every day for the nine of us, and cleaned up after that with some help from her children. The house had to be kept clean, beds made, floors swept, dishes washed and dried, clothes washed and ironed. She had two irons, one on the stove getting hot while she used the second. When it cooled, it went on the stove and she picked up the other one. Clothes were starched and sprinkled to make ironing easier. As the children grew older, they were able to help with that, but there were years when it was all her own work to do. She boiled the bed sheets in a big black pot in the back yard over a fire. She had to lift them out of the boiling water with a long stick because they were too hot for her to hold to wring the water out. They hung on the clothes line, white and clean. I loved to jump in the dry sheets and smell that fresh aroma. She called me to get out of there!

She mentioned one time that she had helped lay out corpses for burial, helped deliver babies, and I know she had all her babies at home with no pain medication. After I was born, she had one more pregnancy that ended in a miscarriage when she fell on the back porch. That almost killed her and her doctor said she would die if she had another pregnancy.

In addition to running the house, watching over her baby chicks, and milking cows, when planting time for the garden came, she also helped plow and plant the vegetables that would be harvested, canned, and preserved for winter meals. My favorite was her pickled beets. She stored the jars under the beds and I remember one season she said, "Now, Polly, this is our last jar for this year." I would have eaten the entire jar right then if I had been allowed.

She canned sometimes in a pressure cooker and we were banned from the kitchen when that was going on. One of her worst fears was that it would explode and someone would be injured. My dad always put on a clean shirt for dinner after washing up from his work of the day and I have thought in my later years of how much laundry she had had to do. Everything was an unending task. Scrub and clean and cook and wash and dry and iron and sew and plow and plant and harvest and can. It seemed that it was work and work and work, never ending. But sometimes I believe my parents thought of those as their happiest years.

One memory is of being in the kitchen with Mama while she seemed to be piddling around and looking out the window at times. The sun had gone down and it was starting to get dark. I looked out the back screen door and Daddy was walking up the back walkway with two rabbits slung over one shoulder and his shotgun on the other. I realized in later years that Mama had been waiting for him to bring home some meat to have for dinner.

The doctor was not called unless it was a matter of life and death. Did you know that drinking water in which peach tree leaves have been soaked will settle a child's upset stomach? My dad always held the glass for us to drink from, so concerned for his children. I remember when I had chicken pox, evidently I never did break out and my temperature rose dangerously. They called the doctor. I was in a bed in the same room where I later watched the fire in the forest. I recovered.

One time my sister, 2 years older than I, ran through the tomato patch and a stick holding up the plants jabbed into her thigh, making a hole in the skin. My parents poured alcohol into it to kill the germs. No doctor was called. She still has a scar on that thigh.

My next to oldest sister, one of one set of twins, had rheumatic fever as a child. I remember the lights on downstairs while I watched at the head of the staircase. They were boiling clothes to put on her legs because of the pain she suffered. She had to go to Vanderbilt Hospital in Nashville for a time. I don't remember what the days were like while she was gone. Daddy went with her. Mama, again, took care of everything at home.

A man came to help Daddy when harvest season came. I won't give you his name to protect his memory. He slept in the attic until my mother ran him into the barn when he urinated out an attic window. My sisters tell me when my parents were on the back porch cutting corn off the cob to be canned, the girls threw the corn cobs at his bald head while he walked toward the barn. He retaliated by getting a switch from a nearby blackberry bush and trying to switch their legs. Daddy always thought he was the one who had been smoking in the woods and threw away a lit cigarette which started the fire that caused him to lose his homestead. Never could be sure about that.

There was a small storage room upstairs in the second rented house. It was like a little attic room where my mother stored her feather beds in the summer. Feather beds, for those who do not recognize the term, are comforters filled with feathers and usually covered with striped ticking. We slept under them in the winter keeping us snug and warm. My parents took all my comics and books away from me because they were afraid I would harm my eyesight by reading too much. I loved to read then and do now. But I sneaked into that little attic room with a flashlight, snuggled into those feather beds, and read everything I could get my hands on.

Daddy started working at the Prisoner of War camp in Crossville as a fireman on 24-hour shifts, one day on and one day off. He earned money for things we needed at home. My mother, again, took care of the home while he was away.

Firemen serving with Robert (Bob) Anderson on far left at Prisoner of War Camp in Crossville, Tennessee. Bob worked 24 hour shifts, one day on and next day off which left him time to farm as well as work.

Christmas was quite an occasion in those days. We had stockings stuffed with nuts, candy, and fruit. Our parents bought bananas by the stalk, apples, and oranges by the bushel, and nuts to crack and dig the good meat out of. The banana stalk was stored in the master bedroom closet to ripen before Christmas. The story goes that someone or more than one someone, sneaked into the closet and not many bananas were left by Christmas.

One Christmas morning we came downstairs and hanging from the light in the center of the living room was the biggest candy cane I ever saw, a foot long and 3/4 inches wide. We took turns passing it back and forth across the room until someone missed and it hit the wall. Candy scattered all over the floor. But we did not let it go to waste and found containers to put it in. That was in the living room where we had no furniture except the dining room chairs spaced along the wall. We had a radio and listened to the Grand Ole Opry on Saturday nights sitting in those chairs. My sisters would sing and dance to the music.

One year my older sister, the one who had rheumatic fever as a child, bought me a doll for Christmas. This was the first Christmas gift I ever had. She and the other girls who were old enough had a job at the local five and dime store and she had her own spending money. She met and married a young man from Crossville so there were only eight of us living in the small duplex we moved to in Oak Ridge.

We had then moved to Oak Ridge, Tennessee. This marriage was not with my father's blessing. Everybody went to school that morning. My sister did not go to school, but boarded a bus to Crossville to meet her boy friend. At the end of the school day, my oldest sister and her boy friend had to tell my parents what had happened. My father took off in his car to chase them down. He went to the parents of the young man and by the time he talked to them, he could better accept the situation. This son-in-law proved to be one of the best of my father's seven sons-in-law.

The Prisoner of War Camp closed after the war but the Atomic City of Oak Ridge, Tennessee, boomed, and Daddy found work there. He commuted at first, but after having a terrible car wreck on the way home one night, he moved his family to Oak Ridge from that huge farm house on the Homesteads in Crossville. The roads he traveled to commute were those narrow, curvy, county roads that existed before the interstate was built.

Houses in Oak Ridge were awarded on some kind of system that had to do with what job the head of the household performed so I understand. The duplex we lived in had 3 small bedrooms, a small living room, and even smaller kitchen where we crowded around the table to eat. My mother moved the washing machine into the living room to do the laundry on weekends. She worked at a day care for a time. Daddy drove her to work early mornings, but her hours ended before his, so she walked home. I know my mother was devastated by the loss of all her living space. She now stored her feather beds under the mattresses on the beds in the summer. They planted a small garden outside under the clothesline space and we all survived. My mother later worked at the school lunchroom where my dad worked and they commuted together.

When Daddy started work in Oak Ridge, he worked at a fire station but when that company closed down he lost that job. He found work with the school system as a custodian. He was assigned to an elementary school and soon was in charge of the other custodians at that school. He kept the hardwood floors shining and the bathrooms sparkling. After a time, he was reassigned to the high school when it was located on the hill at Jackson Square.

Oak Ridge had some heavy snows during those years. One night it snowed what must have been a record. Daddy got up in the early morning hours, drove to the high school, and shoveled the snow off the sidewalks so that the children could get from the school buses to their classrooms without getting their shoes wet. He did not want them to have to walk in the snow.

Later that morning the local newspaper came to the high school with the school superintendent and took pictures of the superintendent shoveling snow from the sidewalk. They had to shovel some snow back onto the sidewalk to make the picture work. My dad was very hurt by that because he felt it looked as though he had not done his job. He took pride in doing his job well, no matter how demeaning it might appear to some.

My parents did buy a home in which they were very comfortable. It had two bedrooms with hardwood floors, a dining room-living room combination with a large enough kitchen to be comfortable for my mother to work in. There was a laundry room where they kept a freezer full of fresh frozen fruit and vegetables. Daddy would go to the peach orchard and pick the best peaches to slice for freezing. Hand-picked strawberries were always on hand from that freezer. Fresh corn, green beans, and okra were always available. I know my mother loved having her own home and enough room to live the way she liked. My mother was a wife and mother to honor. My father was the most honest person I have ever known. I truly appreciate the good character they passed on to their children.

Some of these photographs have been passed down from generation to generation and show family ancestors as well as clothing styles, transportation modes, and life styles lived in the early 1900s and later years.

GRANDPARENTS OF
JAMES CARL ANDERSON AND POLLY PURNELL

"Pa" (Tom) and "Ma" (Polly) Anderson's family photo.

Pictured from left, Dillard, oldest son; Johnny, son (Antioch School Teacher); Pa and Ma Anderson; Effie, only daughter; Evie, Dillard's daughter; Robert (Bob), youngest son; and James Bedford, son, wearing his wide-brim hat.

HOME OF BEDFORD AND LOLA BETTY (LOFTIS) ANDERSON BUILT IN 1926.

The historic 6-room, 3-porch house was built in 1925-1926 by James Bedford Anderson on The Ridge, (today 210 Pap Johnson Circle).

Robert (Bob) Anderson, Bedford's brother, and some farm hands helped build the house on a 100 acre farm. A metal roof has been on the house 86 years and does not leak in 2010.

A family of nine resided in the house. The oldest living child of Bedford Anderson lives there today.

The house has served as a residence, child-care faciity, medical rooming house, temporary funeral home, and boarding house.

The CCC young men occupied rooms in the mid-1930s. Two WWII heroes occupied rooms in the late 1930's and early 1940's (Herman C. Anderson and Tom C. Bennett).

Those who lived in the house decades ago, often visit, sit on the front porch, converse and watch birds, deer, squirrels, rabbits, dogs and cats.

The Johnson String Band (lived across Highway 56) often practiced on the front porch. Bedford played the harmonica. Uncle Henry played banjo. Pneumonia in April, 1936, prevented him from performing on the De Ford Bailey Show (Grand Ole Opry) in Nashville.

GROUP PHOTO OF ANDERSON FAMILY AND DESCENDANTS

Front row left to right: Willard Gailbreath, Clay Anderson, Omer Haile, Doris Anderson, Johnny W. Anderson

Second row left to right: Thomas E. Anderson, Dillard Paul Anderson, Cora Belle Anderson, Virginia (Jackson) Birdwell, Polly Anderson, Roselle Haile, Ogal Allen

Third row left to right: Lorena Anderson, Ruby Anderson, Lyda Anderson, Eva Haile, Lura Gailbreath, Oliver Anderson, Ruby Allen Anderson, Auther Allen, Liddie Anderson Allen

Fourth row left to right: Willie Haile (holding his son) Raymond Jessie Gailbreath

Cora Anderson is holding Mildred Gailbreath (Crymes), Polly Anderson is holding Irene Anderson (Yankee)

James Carl Anderson, Supervisor of Adult Education in
Jackson County, (named after General/President Andrew
Jackson) Tennessee (1987-2008), led his Adult Education
"Americana" Talent Contest Team to a first place finish in
a state-wide contest in Gatlinburg, Tennessee, in 2002.

ANDERSON FAMILY MEMBERS ATTENDING THE
DILLARD ANDERSON FAMILY RE-UNION IN 2002

From left front row – Allene (Anderson) Tribble, Reba
(Anderson) Chambers, Polly (Anderson) Purnell, Elise
Anderson Hall, and Olene Long. Back row from left is Carl
Tribble, Nathaniel (Nat) Chambers, and Ernest Long.

HOME OF CLARENCE ANDERSON

Members of the Anderson family gathered at the Gainesboro home of Clarence Anderson in 2002 for music and fellowship. From back left, Reba (Anderson) Chambers, Polly (Anderson) Purnell, S.W. Forkum, husband of Bonnie (Anderson) Forkum, and James Carl Anderson. From front left, Nathaniel (Nat) Chambers and Clarence Anderson, brother of James Carl.

www.ingramcontent.com/pod-product-compliance
Lightning Source LLC
Chambersburg PA
CBHW052246290526
45785CB00016B/1407